"One cannot but be impressed with the gifts and insight God has given James Spencer for seeking to make an effective entry of Gospel 'seed' into hardened soil. His spirit is not argumentative, yet he is authoritative. There is worthy winsomeness to be cultivated in every Christian witness. May this book's insights contribute to that in us all."

Jack W. Hayford, Senior Pastor
The Church On The Way
Van Nuys, California

"Readable, on target and much needed.... James Spencer challenges Christians to volunteer for service in the war against atheism and pantheism. Here men and women unacquainted with technical philosophical terms can appreciate the importance of presenting a solid case for belief in a personal, moral Creator. This book is *needed*."

Dr. Gordon R. Lewis
Professor of Systematic Theology and
Christian Philosophy
Denver Conservative Baptist Seminary

"*Hard Case Witnessing* is another example of this man's ability to see through the smoke screen of deception and strike a blow for the freedom of those caught in the devil's complex web of lies. This book will prepare God's people to evangelize tough, sophisticated people."

Ed Decker, Founder, *Saints Alive*
Author, *The God Makers*

Also by James R. Spencer

Beyond Mormonism
Have You Witnessed to a Mormon Lately?

Co-authored with Ed Decker

The Mormon Dilemma (video)

HARD CASE WITNESSING

JAMES R. SPENCER

Published by
√ chosen books

FLEMING H. REVELL COMPANY
TARRYTOWN, NEW YORK

Scripture quotations in this publication are from The New King James Version. Copyright © 1979, 1980, 1982 Thomas Nelson, Inc., Publishers.

Library of Congress Cataloging-in-Publication Data

Spencer, James R.
    Hard case witnessing : winning the "impossibles" for Christ /
James R. Spencer.
      p. cm.
    ISBN 0-8007-9179-7
    1. Witness bearing (Christianity)   I. Title.
BV4520.S63 1991
248'.5—dc20
                                        90-22588
                                         CIP

A Chosen book
Copyright © 1991 by James R. Spencer

Chosen Books Publishing Company, Ltd.
Published by Fleming H. Revell Company
Tarrytown, New York
Printed in the United States of America

I dedicate this book with love to:
Margaretta, Jaime, Heather,
Erin and Dave,
Jimmy and Scotty

Acknowledgments

This book has been difficult to write and could not have been completed without the support of many faithful people:

My wife and companion, Margaretta, and my daughters, Jaime and Heather, who sacrificially allow me to invest so much time and energy in my ministry;

Gordon Lewis, who brought focus and direction to the early manuscript;

Dick Landis, who provided many valuable insights, much encouragement, and who challenged me toward clarity;

Tim Moen, who provided faithful support and positive feedback, and who wrote the study questions;

Ed Decker and Bill Schnoebelen and, posthumously, Walter Martin, who constantly remind me of the cost of apologetics;

John Sherrill, who forced me toward precision;

Tim Dart, Jane Campbell and Ann McMath, who did important editorial work;

The many supporters of *Through the Maze* who, as patrons, make it possible for me to continue;

Sonny and Judy Bowman, who hold down the fort;

Jean, Estelle and all who pray for me;

And pastors Dan Ferguson and Tony Maupin who counsel and protect me.

Contents

HARD CASE WITNESSING

Section 1
Identifying Hard Cases

1
Meeting the Hard Cases

Isaac Asimov is a nice guy with dramatic muttonchop whiskers. Once a month this Russian-born (but as he says "Brooklyn-bred") author of more than four hundred books indulges in his secret passion: He sings comic opera with his pals in New York's Gilbert and Sullivan Society.

Asimov is a charming walking encyclopedia. His simple language, humor and warmth delight audiences. He is a man interested in the common good: He is concerned with world hunger, overpopulation and the destruction of the ozone layer.

Asimov is also a secularist, by which I mean someone who seeks to approach life without "the hindrance of religion." He thinks belief in God is at the least irrelevant, and perhaps even harmful. Secularists often refer to themselves as humanists, and this is true of Asimov. As a signer of the Humanist Manifesto II he is convinced that "no deity will save us; we must save ourselves."

Asimov is past president of the American Humanist Association. During his presidency he constantly opposed evangelical Christianity. For Asimov, all evangelicals are "fundamentalists"—narrow-minded, Bible-toting bigots, responsible for most of the world's ills. Asimov dismisses evangelicals as anti-intellectual and dangerous. He likens them to Omar, the Muslim calif, who burned the library of Alexandria saying, "If the books [therein] agree with the Koran, they are not necessary and may be burned; if they disagree with the Koran, they are pernicious and must be burned." Evangelicals "think that all of knowledge will fit into one book called the Bible and refuse to allow that there is even the conceivability of an error in there" (*The Humanist*, January/February 1989).

When men die, Asimov says, they go to neither heaven nor hell. There is only nothingness. His fundamental theory is materialistic: The universe is nothing but matter and matter in motion; no spiritual dimension exists; no super-intellect is behind creation.

Isaac Asimov is what I call a hard case. He is difficult to approach with the Gospel of Jesus Christ because as with all hard cases, he is separated from God by religious or philosophical systems that are alternatives to the message of personal salvation.

Shirley MacLaine is another hard case, but of a different kind. She is probably the last person in the world with whom Isaac Asimov would want to be identified. MacLaine represents everything Asimov despises: all that is unscientific, irrational and spooky-spiritual. Yet MacLaine and Asimov are both effectively isolated from the truth about God by philosophical alternatives to the Gospel.

MacLaine is an occultist, a leader in what we have come to call the New Age movement. Unlike Asimov she does not doubt God's existence. She is very much "into" God. For MacLaine, *everything* is spiritual. While Asimov denies the existence of the spirit realm, MacLaine doubts the existence of the physical world. MacLaine's philosophy stems from the concept of monism: Everything is one spiritual reality; only God exists. The physical universe is an illusion. Our job is to escape the world of illusion—the physical—and *become one* with the true spiritual world, at which point we ourselves become God.

MacLaine, a New Age guru, has written several books detailing her spiritual experiences. Her one-day "Higher Consciousness Seminars" (which *Newsweek*, July 27, 1987, calls "part pep-rally, part séance-in-a-circus-tent") attract thousands of people at $300 a head. She is fascinated with all things psychic and recently praised the metaphysical advances of the Soviet Union. She calls the Russian occult movement "very, very evolved."

For all their differences, MacLaine and Asimov share at least one thing in common: scorn for "fundamentalist" Christians. MacLaine has some room for a mystical brand of Christianity, however, because she senses some Christians "resonate to the highest octave of . . . positive love capacity."

Isaac Asimov believes there is no God; MacLaine believes *everything* is God. Asimov is an atheist, a *material* monist who believes everything is material. MacLaine is a *spiritual* monist who believes everything is spirit. These two ideas challenge classic Christianity from opposite poles. They represent two of the three hard case challenges to the Gospel of Jesus Christ.

The third comes from groups Christians refer to as cults. These are groups that claim a biblical heritage, yet have departed from orthodox Christianity.

Cults have always plagued Christianity. Throughout history thousands of groups have broken away from the Church claiming it has fallen from true faith and that they are the only true Christians. Cults typically retain much of the terminology and doctrine of orthodox Christianity, but redefine the nature and purpose of Jesus Christ.

An example of this counterfeit Christianity is the cult of Sun Myung Moon, founder of the Unification Church. Moon was born to Presbyterian parents in Korea in 1920. He claimed to have had a vision in which Jesus told him to restore true Christianity to the earth. Moon was to finish the job Jesus failed to accomplish. The problem, according to Moon, was that while Jesus won mankind's spiritual redemption, He was crucified before He could marry and have children. As a result, He failed to purify the human race physically. Moon supposedly accomplished that task with his marriage to his fourth wife, Jak Ja Han, in 1960. Though Moon's religion contains occult elements, it is a non-Christian cult because it departs from orthodox Christian teaching.

The Mormon prophet, Joseph Smith, founded Mormonism after a vision in which he, too, was told the Church had fallen and God was calling him to restore it. Mormonism is another example of cultism.

Hard Cases Are Everywhere

Asimov's secularism, MacLaine's occultism and Moon's cultism are examples of hard case philosophies. These alternatives to the Gospel are not, I am quite sure, philosophical accidents. I believe they are purposed, sophisticated and malicious attacks upon scriptural truth about God and man. I am convinced the devil has set himself to pervert the Gospel message through philosophical and religious misunderstanding.

At this point, I want to pause for a moment to describe a problem I face in writing this book. The problem has to do with the use of Scripture in addressing hard cases. We must be careful in our use of the Bible in witnessing. As I have pointed out, secularists scoff at the thought that the Bible is the Word of God. Occultists ridicule the idea that the Bible occupies a unique place among the scores of religious writings found throughout the world. Only the cultist has a regard for the Bible as unique Scripture, but he often thinks that our Bible needs to be rewritten or otherwise edited. We must bear this in mind as we approach these three hard case categories. It would be futile, for example, to refute Asimov and Mac-Laine with quotes from Scripture.

The Bible tells us Satan comes only to steal, kill and destroy (John 10:10). Asimov and MacLaine, however, are unaware that they are deceived. Christians realize that such people are victims of the devil's lies. Millions of people have been robbed of fellowship with God because the devil has thrown them a curve. Though they may be idealistic and have a desire to live honest, righteous lives, they have been spiritually duped. If they are not rescued they face eternal separation from God.

The United States once was a theistic nation. People generally believed that God existed and that man was morally responsible to His laws. This has changed dramatically. Secularism has come to dominate the United States, indeed the entire Western world. Science has become God for many people. By the 1950s intellectuals were glibly declaring "God is dead!"

Nowhere is secularism more observable than on the college campus. My friend Tim's experience is typical. His physics professor, a dyed-in-the-wool secularist, challenged Christianity from the lectern regularly. Like so many young Christians, Tim was not prepared for his teacher's blatant secularism. "Nothing exists," the professor told his class, "except matter and matter in motion. There is no God, no absolute morality, no reason behind the way things are. Man is but the evolutionary product of numberless chance mutations."

Tim, frustrated that a man he highly respected was so devoid of spiritual insight, boldly asked the professor what he lived for if he had no hope for life beyond death. The professor said, "I guess I live from one sexual climax to another."

In the last twenty years secularism has had to compete with occultism for equal time on campuses. In the last ten years we have experienced an explosion of the occult. Schools and churches tout Eastern mystical philosophy; the yellow pages are full of New Age counselors; witchcraft— and even Satanism—is widespread. Evangelical Christians were shocked to learn that President Reagan's appointment schedule was cleared through his wife's astrologer.

The dramatic rise of the occult in America was, in large part, a backlash from the materialistic lifestyle of America following World War II. Idealistic young people who had not experienced the rigors of the Depression and war years were quick to point out inequities and shallowness in American society. They were discouraged by the Vietnam War. They opened their arms to the hippie/drug movement and followed Timothy Leary's suggestion to "tune in, turn on and drop out." Eastern religious philosophy permeated the hippie movement.

Finally, non-Christian cults flourish. Mormonism has baptized five million converts in the last twenty years; Jehovah's Witnesses are at our doors; new aberrant groups spin off from the Church continually under the leadership of earnest but misguided leaders.

Combating the Three-Headed Monster

Evangelical Christians are in continual contact with hard cases and they cannot escape the command of Jesus to win them for His Kingdom. That call is commonly called the Great Commission:

> "Go therefore and make disciples of all the nations, baptizing them in the name of the Father and of the Son and of the Holy Spirit, teaching them to observe all things that I have commanded you."
>
> Matthew 28:19–20

Hard cases are not easily won to Christ. The sad fact is, Christians are not reaching them. It is my observation that if a person in America has not heard and accepted the Gospel message by age eighteen, he or she has heard and accepted an alternative to it.

Many Christians are not prepared to win hard cases. We are too often ignorant of what hard cases believe, intimidated by their polished responses and grossly unprepared in our own Christianity.

Nevertheless, hard cases *can* be won. I have had the privilege of leading Mormons, New Agers and atheists to Christ. I have heard hundreds of testimonies of former secularists, occultists and cultists. In giving us the Great Commission, Jesus did not give us "Mission Impossible."

The Gospel is still "the power of God to salvation for everyone who believes" it (Romans 1:16). We must rise to the challenge of reaching the hard cases. To do that we must equip ourselves for the battle.

Equipping is both spiritual and intellectual. It is necessary to understand how the devil poisons those he has marked for destruction, to know the antidote for the poison and to know how to administer the antidote. As God has revealed Himself to mankind, the devil has opposed it with alternative ideas. We will be tracing that interaction—illustrated on the two charts that follow here—in later chapters. For now keep in mind the two principles that must be balanced constantly by the wise evangelist: truth and love. He must be loving because the truth without love is too hard. He must be tough, on the other hand, because love without the truth is too soft. The Holy Spirit can use a combination of truth and love to win hard cases—"impossibles"—for Christ.

©1990 James R. Spencer

**Chart A:
Pathways of Error**

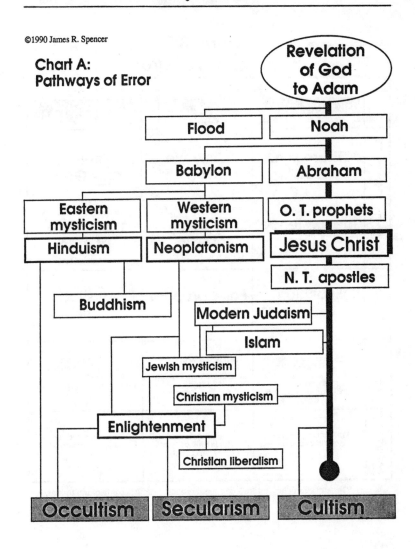

Revelation
of God
to Adam

Flood — Noah

Babylon — Abraham

Eastern mysticism — Western mysticism — O. T. prophets

Hinduism — Neoplatonism — Jesus Christ

N. T. apostles

Buddhism

Modern Judaism

Islam

Jewish mysticism

Christian mysticism

Enlightenment

Christian liberalism

Occultism   Secularism   Cultism

Chart B:
Examples of Error

	Secularism	Cultism	Occultism
M E S S A G E	"There is no God"	"Only we know God"	"There is only God"
E R R O R	The denial of **The existence of God** God is "far off"	The mistake about **The nature of God** Jesus is not fully God	The overestimation of **The nature of man** Man is God
I D O L	Evolution	False prophet or scripture	Mystical experience
G* R O U P S	Secular humanists Atheists Marxists Agnostics Unitarian/Universalists Deists	Jehovah's Witnesses The Way International The Unification Church Islam Modern Judaism	Mormonism Christian Sciences New Age movement Human potential movement Eastern mysticism
R E S P O N S E	Rational arguments against evolution	Scriptural proofs for the full deity of Jesus Christ	Exposing "hidden things of darkness"

*General examples, not limited to these groups. Likewise, some organizations, like Mormonism, fit into more than one category.

2
The Devil's Legacy

It is important to be clear-eyed about the origins and the enormous cost of secularism, occultism and cultism. These three philosophies are born of the devil and their cost to us in terms of misery and alienation is beyond counting. Let's get a clearer picture of Satan himself.

John Milton opened his classic epic poem *Paradise Lost* with an imagined account of Lucifer's fall from heaven. In Milton's story the great archangel is hurled from heaven and lies, with his diabolical cronies, in the lake of fire in hell. After nine days and nights Lucifer begins to speak to his demon friend Beelzebub. Lucifer makes it clear that though he is kicked out of heaven, he is undefeated in spirit. He coldly describes his unrepentant mindset: He will study revenge and hate; he is determined never to yield his "invincible spirit":

> Farewell, happy fields,
> Where joy forever dwells! Hail, horrors! hail,
> Infernal world! and thou, profoundest Hell,
> Receive thy new possessor, one who brings
> A mind not to be changed by place or time.

The mind is its own place, and in itself
Can make a Heaven of Hell, a Hell of Heaven. . . .
Better to reign in Hell than serve in Heaven.

Milton then describes how, in the bitterness of defeat and jealousy, the devil watches as God creates man in the Garden of Eden. Then Satan sets himself to seduce mankind. His purpose is not so much to harm man, but to harm God. The devil, according to Milton, will touch God by touching God's "darling sons."

The Biblical Chronicle of Evil

The Bible says evil originated in the Garden of Eden when the devil tempted man to sin. The devil is tireless in his attack upon mankind. What he began in the Garden of Eden he has repeated throughout history. He seduced Adam and Eve by telling them that disobeying God would not lead to death; rather, they would become like God (Genesis 3:5).

The Garden story is only the beginning of the interaction between the devil and mankind. Theologians ponder why God allows the devil to tempt man. A ready and satisfying answer does not exist, but orthodox Christianity teaches that Satan continues to have access to the minds of men.

Satan's interaction with mankind has left its imprint throughout history. We read in Genesis 4 that he enticed Cain to rise up and kill his brother, Abel. By the end of that same chapter a man named Lamech boasted to his plural wives that he killed a man for merely "hurting" him. By chapter 6, God saw that "every intent of the thoughts of [man's] heart was only evil continually."

Sick of mankind's rebellion, God destroyed the earth by

flood, saving only eight souls. Within a few generations a man named Nimrod built two cities that excelled in evil arts—Nineveh and Babel, also known by its Greek name, Babylon. At Babylon the citizens declared proudly that they would build a tower into heaven and "make a name for themselves." Babylon is symbolic of occultish religion—"mystery" (Revelation 17:5)—and evil in the Bible. It is the "dwelling place of demons, a prison for every foul spirit" (Revelation 18:2).

Evil Ideas Are Wrong Ideas

Devilish ideas, once they are firmly established in the minds of people, lose their fearsome appearance. The philosophical ideas of secularism, occultism and cultism are so widespread as to be commonplace.

Today the world continues to be seduced by the devil. It seems at the end of its tether: Half of all marriages end in divorce; drug addiction is rampant; sexually transmitted disease threatens to bankrupt our health care systems. These and other social ills exist because we have chosen to disregard God's counsel. Destruction and misery mark the way of the people who forsake the Lord (Romans 3:16).

The drug crisis, for example, is the result of a philosophical lie. We were told in the '60s that drugs hurt no one but the user, and that no one should tell anybody else what he can or cannot put into his own body. Yet today our cities are paralyzed by drug addiction and the governments of the Western hemisphere seem impotent in the face of Colombian thugs.

Another philosophical lie of that era was: "If it feels good, do it!" This is the devilish lie that sexual experience is amoral.

Liberated social thinkers told us there were no moral sexual bounds for consenting adults. The rationale of the free love movement was, "What consenting adults do in their bedrooms is nobody else's business." This is plain foolishness. The free love movement was not about love, but about sex. And it was not free, it was tremendously costly. Almost nightly on the news we hear, for instance, about the enormous financial, physical or emotional effects of AIDS.

The Bible adamantly sets the boundary for sexual activity: within marriage—period! When any part of America gives up on God, it throws over His laws. Now to suggest that sexual activity should be confined to marriage is to be branded out of touch with reality. To call homosexuality a sin is to be an insensitive bigot.

No one is so blind as the one who wills not to see. No amount of compassion for those inflicted with AIDS can change the fact that homosexuality (and, secondarily, drug abuse and fornication) is the cause of the AIDS crisis. The disease spreads easily among homosexuals because anal sex causes bleeding. The semen of infected men readily enters the bloodstreams of other men.

Sexual immorality and another tragedy, disdain for marriage, go hand in hand. American society has failed to safeguard the sanctity of marriage. Divorce is now too easy a solution to complex problems. We are a nation of throwaway relationships. The very word *society* becomes meaningless when we make it easy for children to be reared without fathers and solemnize marriages with little hope of effecting their permanence.

Another hallmark of ungodly philosophy is abortion, which costs 1.6 million American children their lives each year. This insanity is rooted in the lie that a human being has no rights until he or she exits the womb. What sophistry allows us to think a fetus has no rights on Monday and is a fully protected citizen on Tuesday, merely by passing through the birth canal? The idea that individuals within a society can practice these ills without harm flies in the face of everything God has revealed to the Judeo-Christian world for thousands of years. Such mistaken ideas originate in the mind of the devil who wants to harm God by harming God's children. They have brought us to the brink of disaster. To fight them—and snatch the lost from the devil's hands—we need to march on the right battlefield. We need to realize that we are in an "idea war" with hell.

By this I mean that the real evil in the world is philosophical. Most people think of evil only in terms of its ultimate manifestation, like the possessed child in *The Exorcist* with her head swiveling around backward. But the Black Masses and human sacrifices of Satanism are actually the manifestations of evil *doctrines*. Hitler's death camps were the outworking of Nazi thinking; Stalin's gulags, the ultimate expression of Communism. Communism is evil because its *ideas* are evil. As I watch the fall of Communism in Eastern Europe, I hope the materialism that built it will fall as well; the economic failure is only the manifestation of the spiritual failure. Without faith in God, a different political structure will be only cosmetic.

Spiritual Warfare

Our battle is against evil ideas. This is where we must start in order to win the hard cases. The devil has used every seductive philosophy he can imagine. Jesus said Satan is the father of lies. His tools are lies and he was a murderer from the beginning (John 8:44).

Thus, the apostle Paul tells us that we war not against flesh and blood, but against "principalities, against powers, against the rulers of the darkness of this age, against spiritual hosts of wickedness in the heavenly places" (Ephesians 6:12). Only Jesus can rescue us from "this present evil age" (Galatians 1:4).

The process for deliverance is the preaching of the Gospel. Salvation occurs when anyone hears the Gospel and believes it (Romans 10:10, 14).

There are hundreds of thousands—millions—of people today, hard cases, who are prevented from hearing the Gospel message. *Actively* prevented. The apostle Paul said: "If our gospel is veiled, it is veiled to those who are perishing, whose minds the god of this age has blinded" (2 Corinthians 4:3–4). The apostle John labels these two opposing sides "the spirit of truth and the spirit of error" (1 John 4:6).

In God's wisdom, He has sent puny mankind up against the devil to rescue those in Satan's power. But He has not sent us powerless. As Martin Luther said, our God is a mighty fortress who has given us the Spirit and gifts. Paul tells us something of our spiritual weapons:

> The weapons of our warfare are not carnal but mighty in God for pulling down strongholds, casting down arguments and every high thing that exalts itself against the knowledge of God, bringing every thought into captivity to the obedience of Christ. 2 Corinthians 10:4–5

Satan opposes us with strong arguments. We face his lies with God's revealed truth. Witnessing to hard cases is a work of reason and Holy Spirit-anointed argument. And the sword of the Spirit, the Word of God, is alive, powerful and sharp (Hebrews 4:12).

With God's help we will pull the devil's fingers out of his victims' ears and uncover their eyes. They will "know the truth," just as Jesus said, "and the truth shall make [them] free" (John 8:32).

3
The Call to Evangelism

Anyone who takes the Great Commission seriously discovers the reality of spiritual warfare. Our primary warfare against the devil occurs at various levels of intensity as we try to implement the Commission. Evangelism takes on at least three forms: relational, declarational and confrontational.

Relational Evangelism

Relational evangelism starts when we get a burden for the soul of an unsaved person. It may be a friend, a relative or someone we encounter in day-to-day business. The Holy Spirit moves in our hearts and causes us to notice someone as a candidate for the Kingdom of God. If we never get such "impressions," it is useful to pray that God would give us a burden for souls. Relational evangelism takes the form of establishing lines of communication that God may choose to use to deliver the Gospel. You may be moved with compassion as you see a street person, a harried waitress, a sales clerk or a passing angry motorist. Perhaps it begins to occur to you that your next-door neighbor is not a Christian and that realization begins to trouble you.

This form of evangelism may begin with just a smile or a kind word. It may include welcoming neighbors into your home or taking them to church where the pastor or others develop the encounter further. Sometimes this kind of evangelism will be simply praying for that person.

Lloyd Jones' conversion is an example of relational evangelism at work. Lloyd was a final-stage drunk. I had met his wife, Cheryl, in a little church in Idaho shortly after she became a Christian. Cheryl asked me to pray for Lloyd. Many Christians began to pray for Lloyd.

Jonesy (as we have since come to call him) was enraged by Cheryl's conversion. He "hated" the Christian people with whom she now associated. He phoned her pastor and told him if he ever met him on the street he would kill him. One night Jonesy came home in a rage with a chain saw, determined to cut their mobile home in half—his idea of a property settlement. Failing to get the saw started, he tucked a gun into his belt and headed out to his pickup. Suddenly he couldn't see to drive. Something was in his eyes. He pulled off the road and found to his amazement that he had an uncontrollable desire to pray. But he didn't know where to begin. He drove to the pastor's house, walked in, dropped to his knees and was saved and delivered of alcoholism immediately. The very next day he was back in the bars—this time to witness to his alcoholic friends about the saving power of Jesus. He hasn't had a drop to drink in fifteen years.

Declarational Evangelism

Ron Rearick was evangelized through a process of declarational evangelism. This form requires us to interact in an immediate way with the prospective Christian. In declarational evangelism we "share our faith." Declaration can take many forms: It can be by verbal testimony or through the delivery of a tract or book. It is at best the result of prayer and accompanied by an anointing of the Holy Spirit.

Sometimes, as in Ron Rearick's case, declarational evangelism involves a bold witness. Ron was a Mafia enforcer known as "the Ice Man." His life of crime led him to try to extort a million dollars from United Airlines by threatening to blow up one of their flights. Ron got 25 years in the federal prison on McNeil Island, Washington.

One day in prison an old convict walked up to Ron and said, "Rearick, you can learn a lot of things in here. You can learn counterfeiting. You can learn safecracking. Or," he said, shoving a Bible in Ron's stomach, "you can get smart." Ron had never been to church, never prayed, never read the Bible, but he couldn't get the old con's words out of his mind. Two nights later in his cell Ron knelt, prayed and was born again. Later when Ron was released he became a full-time evangelist. Ron Rearick responded to declarational evangelism, just as Lloyd Jones had to relational evangelism.

Confrontational Evangelism

Confrontational evangelism puts us in a still more interactive mode, and will be the focus of this book. Confrontational evangelism employs the theological concept known as apologetics. Apologetics simply means we are making a reasoned argument (*apologia* in Greek) for or against a particular idea. It is what Peter had in mind when he said, "Always be ready to give . . . a reason *[apologia]* for the hope that is in you" (1 Peter 3:15).

Confrontational evangelism occurs when we engage in dialogue with people in an attempt to convince them of the truth and relevance of the Gospel message. Perhaps we encounter a person, for instance, who desires to become a Christian but believes he must first give up all his bad habits. We would explain the doctrine of salvation by grace until he understood he could come to Christ immediately, without first becoming "good enough." We confront his misunderstanding of salvation with the Bible's teaching on the subject.

Such confrontations are not always comfortable. I was approached at a dinner party once by a Hindu who knew I was a Christian minister. He was somewhat aggressive in his pronouncement that "Christians foolishly preach there is only one God when, in fact, the Bible teaches there are many gods." He held that opinion because the First Commandment says, "Thou shalt have no other gods before me." His argument was, "If God wants us to have no other gods before Him, then He is admitting the existence of other gods." My job was to explain that the Bible teaches monotheism, the existence of only one God. Though men may enshrine demons as gods (that's what the First Commandment refers to), that does not *make* them gods.

Confrontational evangelism can be especially rewarding. I talked once with a disillusioned Mormon who had turned to a New Age religion after leaving Mormonism. The one thing Jerry remembered from Mormonism was that the Bible "was the Word of God insofar as it is translated correctly." That doctrinal statement is contained in Mormonism's Eighth Article of Faith. Jerry was searching for God, but couldn't hear much from his Christian friends because he was convinced their source of information about God—the Bible—was unreliable. His Christian friends continued to tell him about their experience with Christ, and he was impressed and intrigued by what they said, but he could not get past his established notion that Christian thought was founded in a document that was little more than a collection of good ideas.

My job with Jerry was to present logical reasons why I believe God not only inspired the Bible, but preserved it. I gave him "a reason for the hope" I have in the Bible. Jerry was impressed enough to begin attending church. Soon he committed his life to Christ. The imperative nature of this kind of apologetic evangelism came home to me two months later when he drowned in a fishing accident.

Apologetic or confrontational evangelism is necessary because many Americans are not only lost spiritually, but also effectively insulated from the Gospel message by the sophisticated arguments against it. The devil has indeed blinded their minds.

Francis Schaeffer, in his book *The Great Evangelical Disaster*, pointed out that America is a post-Christian society. Chuck Colson, in his book *Against the Night*, calls our time "the new Dark Ages." These statements underscore the spiritual poverty of our age.

Americans once, by and large, believed in a God who was "near," interacting with the universe He made. He had a plan to rescue fallen humans. Today, more often than not, Americans are unlikely to believe man needs to be rescued. Most Americans are secularists; they believe man is a product of evolution, in charge of his own destiny. If he needs anything at all, he will find it within himself.

If we are to reach American secularists, we will have to confront their doubts about the very existence of God. It is pointless to talk to them about Jesus, the Son of a God they don't believe in. How interested can they be in exploring

Bible verses if they do not believe in a God who spoke through the prophets? *We must reach them where they are.*

If secularists are to be reached with the message of Christ, they must first become convinced that God exists and that He expects something of them. As the writer of Hebrews stated, "He who comes to God must believe that He is, and that He is a rewarder of those who diligently seek Him" (Hebrews 11:6). We will reach the secularist when we confront him or her logically about the evidence for God's existence.

Likewise, the occultist needs to be confronted. He believes man is God or may become God. His world view is entwined in twisted mysticism. Just as the Old Testament prophets and New Testament apostles confronted the gods of the pagans, so must we. When New Agers put their trust in magic, witchcraft and the "god nature within us," we must tell them lovingly that idolatry and ceremony are powerless to save them. Occult practices obscure—they do not clarify—the nature of God. We must expose the hidden things of shame in order that occult practitioners may turn to the light.

Cultists, too, need to be confronted. The cultist is convinced that his group alone knows anything about God. They think they have the fuller and deeper insight into the Bible and they preach another Jesus who lacks the full divinity required to save man from his sins. We will be learning the apologetics needed to reach all three groups.

For most Christians, the challenge of confrontational evangelism is a difficult one. We Christians have often been unwilling to transfer the concept of tough love into the arena of witnessing. Worse, we have believed the propaganda of the enemy: that loving our friends means we never confront them about eternal destiny. Sometimes we even boast that we never discuss politics or religion.

For me, this is a grave mistake. When we say we love people too much to confront them with the demands of their Creator, we miss the point. It is like saying, "If my neighbor's house were on fire, I'd love him too much to tell him." It would be like a medical doctor who found a spot on a lung X-ray and justified his failure to tell because he loved his patient too much to confront him with the truth. The cost? Our neighbor's house burns down. He dies of cancer. He goes to hell.

On the hopeful side, Christians are beginning to learn we have to take tough stands on issues. We are learning that in all interpersonal relationships there is a need for "tough love."

Dr. Walter Martin, eminent cult expert, used to say, "The cults are the unpaid bills of the Church." It is time to rise and pay those bills. I humbly offer Spencer's Two Generalized Laws for reaching secularists, cultists and occultists:

1. We need apologetics only if we are dealing with hard cases.

2. If they are over eighteen, they are all hard cases.

4
The Call to Hard Case Witnessing

The ancient Greek philosophers discovered that three elements were required to win someone to an intellectual position: *ethos*, *pathos* and *logos*. *Ethos* means that those with whom we dialogue see us as ethical; we are believable, our motives are seen as pure. *Pathos* means we are seen as caring about the persons with whom we are discussing our differences; they perceive us as genuinely interested in their well-being, not simply interested in winning an argument or gaining a convert. *Logos* means the proposition we are espousing is logical, factual and viable; we have truth on our side. When all three of these elements come together, people are most likely to believe what we are saying and accept our proposition.

Those who choose to engage in hard case witnessing must examine their motives. Any motive other than a sincere desire to see someone reconciled to God in Christ will be quickly recognized. Those who confront error out of anger or frustration are doomed to the further frustration of seeing their message obscured. Our arguments must, therefore, include both truth and love. We must "always be ready to give a defense . . . *with meekness and fear*" (1 Peter 3:15).

No matter how right our motives are, they will often be seen with suspicion. Obviously, those the devil holds captive will find us threatening, unloving and self-serving. Cultists, for example, tend to be paradoxically blind: When they proselytize Protestants and Catholics, they are exercising their religious liberty; but when we evangelicals approach *them*, we are attacking them. I'm always amazed that the Mormon Church, for example, feels persecuted when it is targeted by evangelicals. Yet Mormonism fields more than 40,000 full-time missionaries to approach Protestants and Catholics because Mormon scripture says "all other churches are wrong, all their creeds are abominable and all their professors are corrupt."

The most difficult opposition for the apologetic evangelist, however, comes not from those to whom he is sent by God to evangelize, but from other Christians. Remarkably, those who seek to win converts to Christ from secularism, occultism and the cults will often be resisted by fellow Christians! This troublesome opposition stems from three primary sources:

• First, too many would-be confrontational evangelists have conducted themselves insensitively; they come on too strong and establish their points mainly through emotion, rather than logic.

• Second, as I have stated, confrontation is inherently painful. Many people who want to avoid confrontation are threatened when they see witnessing activities they view as embarrassing and are fearful to emulate them.

• Third, in our pluralistic society, many Christians assume a person's right to religious freedom means that he can never be challenged. We must not lose our Master's own perspective. Christianity is not one of several good ideas about God. Jesus Himself clearly declared He is the *only* way to God. He has called us to go into every nation and make disciples. As Christ's ambassadors, we must witness to Him in spite of the world's protests.

The Risk of Being Misunderstood

As we witness to hard cases, we must never lose sight of the fact that we are in a spiritual battle led by a sophisticated, tireless opponent. The devil opposes everything we do in an attempt to frustrate us and weary us, to defeat us in order to prevent us from accomplishing our goal of liberating those he has deceived.

We may not want to fight error, but those of us who are called to this battle must go. The apostle Jude said he preferred to write about the Christian's common salvation in Christ, but he "found it necessary" to challenge Christians to "contend earnestly for the faith which was once for all delivered to the saints." This he had to do because ungodly men had crept into the Church preaching heresy.

Walter Martin, the late apologist, exemplified a man who continued steadfast in his opposition to error. I knew Walter to be gentle and sensitive, listening patiently to individuals as a minister of Christ. But Walter was also able to mount compelling arguments with gusto because he knew men's souls were at stake. Once when Walter was on a TV talk show the host handed him a card, just as the cameras came on, that said, "Please don't mention Mormonism, Jehovah's Witnesses or Christian Science." Walter was shocked by the directive. Looking into the camera, he said, "I am an expert in Mormonism, Jehovah's Witnesses and Christian Science. Presumably that is why I have been invited to be on this show. Now I have just been handed a card and asked not to mention those groups." Turning to the woman host he asked, "Why is that?"

She rose to the challenge by saying, "Because it's so *negative*. Jesus was never negative!"

Walter said, "Well, I disagree with you and if you'll give me two minutes I'll tell you why." Walter then recited excerpts from Jesus' continuing and blistering attacks on the Pharisees, calling them "whited sepulchers, serpents, graves covered over, children of hell, sons of the devil" and other equally distasteful epithets.

When he finished she said, "Well, could you at least *smile* when you say it?"

Walter said, "Sure." And, smiling widely, proceeded to go through the list again in its entirety. When he was through, they were both laughing and he had made the point that Jesus was relentless in the face of religious error.

Christians frequently feel uncomfortable in the presence of confrontive ministry. Once, after D. L. Moody preached a particularly fiery sermon, a listener—a Christian—came up to him and said, "Brother Moody, I don't like the way you get people to come to Christ." He objected to Moody's graphic portrayal of hell and the immediacy of the judgment.

"I don't much like it myself," Moody said. "How do you get people to come to Christ?"

"Well, I don't have a method."

"Then," said Moody, "I don't like mine *less* than I don't like yours!"

A special reluctance to accept hard case witnessing is evident in the Church today. Apologists often find themselves misunderstood. I can remember when my friend Ed Decker, founder of Saints Alive! and co-author (with Dave Hunt) of

The God Makers, was canceled from a television show because the owner of the network said he did "not want to offend my Mormon viewers." This is an example of "foggy thinking." As noted seminary professor Howard Hendricks says, "A mist in the pulpit is a fog in the pew." I am fearful that we are not preparing Christians with adequate doctrinal foundations. If that is true, not only will they be unable to win their neighbors, they are in danger of falling to the devil's deception themselves.

Paul and Hard Cases

When I think of apologetic witnessing, I think immediately of the apostle Paul, doubtless the world's greatest evangelist. I think of his confronting the Epicurean nature worshipers and Stoic pantheists on Mars Hill in Athens. He quoted their own poets and directed the conversation to their foundational world view. Recognizing these men as secularists, he did not quote one verse from the Old Testament, but reasoned with them about the evidence for God from nature. He held his own so well with them that they were impressed enough to listen to him tell of Christ's redemption. It is true that "some mocked." But others said, "We will hear you again on this matter." A woman named Damaris, a philosopher named Dionysius and several others—in the midst of this spiritual warfare—believed Paul and accepted Christ (Acts 17:16–34).

Likewise, in Corinth, Paul went to the synagogue every Sabbath and reasoned with the Jews and Greeks. He was "constrained by the Spirit, and testified to the Jews that Jesus is the Christ." When they blasphemed he "shook his garments and said to them, 'Your blood be upon your own heads;

43

I am clean.' " Nevertheless, in the heat of those arguments, Crispus, the ruler of the synagogue, was won to Christ and Paul established what would eventually become a great church (Acts 18:4–8).

In Ephesus Paul reasoned and persuaded in the synagogue for three months and reasoned daily in the school of Tyrannus for two years. He disrupted the whole city, burning witchcraft books in the center of town, and so disturbed the idolatry and trafficking in idols that the priests of the temple of Diana tried to have him prosecuted. A riot ensued and Paul barely escaped with his life (Acts 19:8–10, 19–40). In Ephesus, too, Paul established a mighty work for God.

Paul not only believed in confrontation, he exhorted others to it. His admonition to the young minister Timothy was: "Preach the word! Be ready in season and out of season. Convince, rebuke, exhort, with all longsuffering and teaching" (2 Timothy 4:2).

Paul said Christian leaders must hold "fast the faithful word as he has been taught, that he may be able, by sound doctrine, both to exhort and convict those who contradict" (Titus 1:9).

The Biblical Mandate

Hard case witnessing has always required a reasonable declaration of the faith. More often than not, that reasoned statement is delivered in the face of a devilish philosophy. The Bible is replete with examples of hard case witnessing:

• Jesus demonstrated a tough, confrontational ministry, especially when encountering the religious errors of groups like the Pharisees. He warned us that in the last days false christs will come in His name to deceive many. Employing great signs and wonders, these false prophets will deceive even the elect if God doesn't bring the world to an end. (See Matthew 24:5, 24.)

● Peter condemned false teaching and false teachers emphatically, saying they, like "natural brute beasts made to be caught and destroyed, speak evil of the things they do not understand. . . . They promise . . . liberty," he said, but "they themselves are slaves." They "secretly bring in destructive heresies." (See 2 Peter 2:1, 12, 19.)

● John warned that an antichrist spirit was in the world, which would rise up from within the Church. False prophets would introduce a "spirit of error." (See 1 John 2:18–19; 4:1–6.)

● Jude said he was compelled to urge believers to contend for the faith because certain men had crept into the Church who served only themselves and attempted to take advantage of Christians. (See Jude 3–4, 12, 16.)

● And on the issue of false doctrine Paul warned repeatedly of the threat: "After my departure savage wolves will come in among you, not sparing the flock. Also from among yourselves men will rise up, speaking perverse things, to draw away the disciples after themselves" (Acts 20:29–30). To the young minister Timothy, Paul said: Charge men that they should teach "no other" doctrine, because "the Spirit expressly says that in latter times some will depart from the faith, giving heed to deceiving spirits and doctrines of demons." (See 1 Timothy 1:3; 4:1.)

Winning hard cases is a difficult assignment. Rising to the challenge takes courage, but the reward of seeing a hard case come to Christ is immense, as is the relief of the one reached. As one woman exiting a cult said to me: "Pastor Spencer, when the scales fell off my eyes, I heard them hit the floor!"

Let's look more deeply at how we can help replace bondage with liberation.

Section 2
Understanding Hard Cases

5
Approaching Hard Cases

To approach secularists, cultists and occultists, we must first differentiate them more completely than we have done so far. This is imperative because we cannot approach everyone in exactly the same way.

But how are we to decide if we are dealing with a secularist? a cultist? an occultist? What if we are talking to people who are eclectic—that is, people who have taken parts and pieces from one or more of our three groups? Our first step is to identify the distinguishing marks of each group.

Identifying the Secularists

Secularists, broadly speaking, are those who believe that God—if He exists at all—is far away and irrelevant to mankind's problems. For our discussion, I want to identify three classes of secularists: atheists, agnostics and what I call practical atheists.

• Atheists are defined as people who deny the existence of God. Madeline Murray O'Hair is the spokesperson of one group of atheists in America. She maintains that belief in God is dangerous and the root of all kinds of evil.

• Agnostics are people who say they do not know if God exists. Many agnostics argue from the philosophical position that since God cannot be proven to exist, nobody knows if He does. For evangelistic purposes agnostics may be treated as atheists.

• Practical atheists, by my definition, are those who profess some level of faith in God, but *act as though* God is far from them. One example of such people are the Unitarian/Universalists. Many Unitarians refer to themselves as deists, that is, people who say God created the universe but has now withdrawn from it.

Most practical atheists are the ones we think of as worldly. They want little to do with God. "It's O.K. for you," they will say, "but it isn't for me." They may be pursuing a lifestyle they know is far from godly. Even if they say, "Sure, I believe in God," they often live as though He were irrelevant. The point is, regardless of their theological profession, their lives are ordered around the belief that God is absent. That, for practical purposes, equals the atheistic position.

Another example of a practical atheist is the liberal Christian. By that I mean the professing Christian for whom God has become distant. I have talked to pastors of mainline Christian churches who are unsure of the deity of Christ, who would not refer to the blood of Christ as meaningful and who rarely consult the Bible for inspiration or guidance. Whenever I am approached by a woman after one of my seminars who begins the conversation with, "My husband is a Christian, but he doesn't want anything to do with the Church. . . ." I begin to guess she is talking about a man who has decided that God is irrelevant. This person may profess a faith in God, but it is a dead faith. The Bible says, "Faith without works is dead" (James 2:20).

Faith is not some mental assertion of the past; it is a living, dynamic relationship with God. With it, one is saved; without it, one is not saved. Any person for whom God is a distant intellectual concept does not have saving faith: "Without faith it is impossible to please Him, for he who comes to God must believe that He is, and that He is a rewarder of those who diligently seek Him" (Hebrews 11:6).

Identifying the Occultists

The bane of mankind is pagan religion. From the first the devil has seized upon the selfishness in the heart of fallen mankind. The Bible persistently explains the wickedness of human nature, points out the penalty for sin and offers redemption through the sacrifice of Christ. The devil, on the other hand, says nothing is wrong with human nature. It is basically good. In fact, it is basically godly. All that is required is to learn unholy secret mystical knowledge and man can become a supreme human entity and, eventually, a god or one with God.

When I use the word *mysticism* in this context I mean the attempts to elevate the soul to sublime heights through secret information, ritual, obedience or extremes of sacrifice. This kind of unholy mysticism is typical of the occultist. In Hinduism, man attempts through religious practice to escape the wheel of death and rebirth; in the most lurid pagan religions, the devotee trades his soul for wealth, power or fleshly gratification; in all cases, the occultist gives himself to the study and practice of a spiritual methodology designed to empower and exalt himself.

Occultism, as I mentioned earlier, began in Babylon and spread throughout the earth. God overcame the heathen in the Promised Land and established Israel. After the incarnation of Christ, Christianity defeated paganism for a season in the Western world but later paganism threatened the Church on many fronts. In the disenchantment of materialism following World War II, idealistic Western youth welcomed Eastern mysticism in the teachings of various gurus. Earlier waves of Eastern religion had penetrated the Church in the liberalism of the Enlightenment (and indirectly in Freemasonry) and in the Theosophical and Christian Science movements of the nineteenth century.

The secularist is identified by his disinterest in God; the occultist is identified by his obsession and fascination with the spiritual world.

The occultist sees Jesus as peripheral. Jesus may be an Ascended Master or a great teacher, but He is one of many expressions of God. Ultimately all occultists believe Jesus is merely a man who possessed information and spiritual power that anyone may possess who applies himself to the study and ritual of the occult.

The cultist, on the other hand, places Jesus (though an unbiblical Jesus) at the center of his faith.

Identifying the Cultists

The word *cult* refers to a subgroup. It is not necessarily a negative word. The so-called "heavy metal" cult simply identifies a group of people who center their attention on a specific brand of music. A personality cult centers around a personality.

For the broader Christian Church, however, the word *cult* has a more negative connotation. It is used to describe one of numerous groups that hover around the true Church, that use the term Christian but preach a different gospel, spirit or Jesus. (See 2 Corinthians 11:4.) In that sense, the Church often assigns the word *cult* to a particular sect.

Perhaps at this point, a proper definition of the term "Christian Church" is in order. The Church is the name Jesus uses for those who are His own by faith. The Church is the organization made up of all who have become Christians—both those now living and those dead. The "one true Church" can only, in the final analysis, be identified by Christ Himself. *He* knows those who have become His through faith. We cannot see into a person's heart.

In the context of this understanding of the word *Church*, many attempts have been made to set up guidelines to identify cults. Cults are usually formed around a strong personality; they are usually authoritarian and they often introduce extrabiblical teaching as Scripture. Sometimes they overemphasize a legitimate Christian doctrine or practice; this generally obscures the larger view of Christ and His redemptive work.

Cults are numerous, can vary widely from each other, may subscribe to many correct doctrines and often use Christian terms. All this, plus the fact that new ones spring up constantly, makes them difficult to classify. We will discuss general categories of identification later in chapters 12 and 13.

There is, however, one central characteristic of cults that I would like to mention here.

It is true that the Bible allows for diversity in the Body of Christ (1 Corinthians 12:4–6, 12–27), but one area is inviolate: that is, the divine nature of Jesus Christ. From the earliest days of the Church, the apostles and elders understood that any internal attack on the Church or deviation from her beliefs centered on this issue.

The central declaration of the Church is "Jesus is Lord." Anything that diminishes His deity is a threat to the Church. In unhealthy subgroups of Christianity, Jesus is retained as head of the Church without being fully God. The early Christian councils focused on forming theological statements to stress that Jesus is both fully God and fully man. Wherever that understanding has slipped—when Jesus' full divinity has been doctrinally jettisoned—the result is spiritual poverty and eventual separation from the Body of Christ.

It is this separation that, in the final analysis, identifies the cults. The ultimate sin of heresy is found in the root meaning of the word *heresy:* "a splitting." Heresy about who Jesus is breaks Christian fellowship. Don't mistake that breaking as the act of the orthodox Church. The heretics leave the Church. In retrospect, the Church identifies them and recognizes their departure:

> Little children, it is the last hour; and as you have heard that the Antichrist is coming, even now many antichrists have come, by which we know that it is the last hour.
>
> They went out from us, but they were not of us; for if

they had been of us, they would have continued with us;
but they went out that they might be made manifest,
that none of them were of us.   1 John 2:18–19

The cults ultimately refuse the clear Bible teaching that
Jesus Christ is God incarnate—God come in the flesh (see
John 1:1, 14; 1 John 4:1–3). By understanding the real, biblical nature of Jesus Christ, we will be able to spot the counterfeit. As a young Christian, I visited a college town in
Montana on business. In a restaurant I noticed a group of
young people having a Bible discussion at a nearby table. As
I heard Bible terms and phrases, I assumed these were Christian brothers. Since I was alone in town I thought they might
direct me to a Bible study or church service. When I approached them they were friendly and invited me to join
them. At first I was pleased with my good fortune in finding
"brothers" so quickly. But after a few minutes I began to hear
things that troubled me. It dawned on me finally that they did
not believe in the Trinity. That doctrine was, they said, an
invention of Constantine and unbiblical.

It turned out that these young people were members of
The Way International, which is viewed by evangelical Christians as a cult. I knew nothing of The Way, but within mo-
ments of encountering their doctrine I knew something was
wrong. Fortunately, I had studied the nature of God from a
biblical perspective before this encounter. Unfortunately, I
was not well enough prepared to affect their thinking. Still, I
am glad I was informed enough to avoid being trapped in a
theological position that could only have stunted my early
Christian growth.

Tactics for the Encounter

Once God has led us into dialogue with a hard case and once we have decided to attempt to witness to him, we need to have a plan in mind. It helps to consider the following points:

1. Is my heart right in this matter?
2. Can I enhance the setting for the discussion?
3. Am I prepared to give an answer for the hope I have?

Is my heart condition right?

We can never check our motives too often. If we find ourselves motivated by anything other than compassion for the soul of our friend, we need to get right before God before we proceed. If I am angry, for example, then I should either get control of myself or avoid the conversation.

Can I improve the setting of the conversation?

Nothing, I find, hinders communication more than having people present who are not helpful. I am often accosted by people after a seminar meeting. Many times a crowd gathers. This is usually not a good setting for a discussion. In the first place, it is much more difficult to be objective if you are being observed. Nobody wants to look bad in front of an audience. Recently a very gentle Mormon bishop talked to me after a meeting. As soon as I sensed his spiritual meekness, I excused myself from the others, led him to a side room and there had a fruitful conversation.

One way to control the setting is to set up an appointment for later. If I find myself in an uncomfortable setting, I will say something like, "I want to continue this discussion, but this isn't a good time for me. Could we set up an appointment?" Then press for a time and a place. When you do that, it is good to make sure you know who will be coming to the appointment. If you are witnessing to a Latter-day Saint, for example, you might be surprised when he shows up with a couple of missionaries who are spoiling for a fight. If that is going to happen, you might want to know about it in advance. To determine this you simply ask, "Will you be coming by yourself?"

By controlling the setting, you can arrive at the meeting with materials that may enhance the discussion. Often these kinds of discussions turn into a number of teaching meetings. (I met with a Moonie missionary for two years before she accepted Christ.)

Am I prepared to give an answer for the hope I have?

You will, of course, never be as prepared as you want to be. We will always feel somewhat inadequate. But we need to begin somewhere. Nothing develops witnessing skills more than actually witnessing. We need to remember that the Holy Spirit will accompany us. He will recall passages of Scripture we didn't know we knew. How many times have I heard Christians say, when describing such encounters, "The Lord led me through the conversation"?

But there will be times when you are in over your head and you know it. At such times honesty is essential—and effective. It's never wrong to say, "I can't answer your questions, but I will do some research. Let's talk again." It may be helpful to give the individual a book or tape. A number of ministries work hard to create books, tracts and audio and videotapes that we can hand to someone and let the material do its work. Ed Decker and I joined together to produce the video "The Mormon Dilemma" expressly so people could hand it to a Mormon and say, "Look at this and tell me what's wrong with it."

Strategy for the Encounter

Our strategy is simply to identify our candidate and present him with information that will undermine the effect of the philosophical lie he has believed. The rest of this book is a compilation of material to help you encounter hard cases. Each section gives you specific information that, within the context of your own personality, will be useful in winning secularists, occultists and cultists.

We will be examining each of the three great groups of spiritual counterfeits in detail. For now, let me make three statements:

1. We confront the secularists with *evidence against the theory of evolution*. The secularist is trying to operate within a world view that excludes God or reduces Him to a minimal, practical role. The secularist world is basically a material (non-spiritual) world. We want, therefore, to weaken the foundation of materialism by combating the theory of evolution, which teaches there is no spiritual creation. Our hope is that he will then be forced to consider at least a theistic world view, which acknowledges God but believes Him to be separated from the world. From a new foundation of theism, the presentation of the Gospel of Christ becomes possible.

2. We confront the occultist's message, "Everything is God," with *a demonstration of the uniqueness and supremacy of Jesus Christ*. We expose the inadequacy of occultic ritual and ceremony to address mankind's sin.

3. We confront the cultist's erroneous explanation of the nature of God with *scriptural evidence for the deity of Christ*. The cultist already uses the Bible in one form or another but he has undermined its authority with additional scripture or the revelation of the cult's prophet. Nevertheless, the Bible can be used. None of the cults effectively eradicates the influence of the Bible.

We must always remember we are combating error with truth, but the error has set up a prejudice against the truth. Hard cases are skeptical of evangelical Christians. They often feel threatened by us.

Let me illustrate our strategy with two stories. Imagine the hard case as living out his life on a luxury liner. That ship represents his world view, his philosophy or religion, and he believes it is safe. Now imagine the Bible-believing Christian rowing up to him in a lifeboat. The hard case looks with disdain at the lifeboat. Why should he leave his elegantly crafted ship to get into the lifeboat? He will not, unless he has good reason to do so. In order to get him off the liner we must take him below decks and show him the holes below the water line. Only when he sees his ship will not save him will he be interested in getting into our simple little boat.

A second example. When I was a young man I bought four recapped tires for my car. Later a friend told me they were no good. He suggested I get rid of them and buy some new ones. But they looked good to me; they had plenty of tread and the car handled well with them. On a trip from California to Wyoming, however, every one of the tires lost its tread. It is a true wonder I wasn't killed.

That's what we are up against with someone who has believed a false doctrine. He doesn't *believe* it is a good idea. He doesn't want another to replace it. The only way I could have been spared the near disaster of having my tires disintegrate would have been to take my tires off my car, put them on a bench and examine them closely. Only then could I have seen the flaws. That is exactly what the apologist must do to win someone who is riding on dangerous spiritual tires.

Sales and Management

We need to remember we are in sales and God is in management. Only God, by His Spirit, can convert people to Himself. We are just messengers. Our job is not to get people saved, but to preach the Gospel as inventively and intelligently as we can.

Secularism, occultism and cultism have this in common: They were devised by Satan as alternatives to the Gospel. The devil spread his lies from the Garden of Eden, through Babylon, up the Indus Valley, through medieval Europe. He infiltrated the Church with Neoplatonism in Enlightenment Europe to secularize the Church. He seduced the ignorant quasi-Christian founders of the great American cults in the spawning ground of New England. Today he has resurrected Eastern paganism in America in the New Age movement as Hinduism bathes us with the occult.

I believe it is vital for us to get a picture of these satanic streams that form the mighty three-headed river of secularism, cultism and occultism. The Bible says we are not to be ignorant of the devil's wiles (2 Corinthians 2:11). Only if we have at least a passing familiarity with the history of evil can we recognize the devil's latest attacks. There is "nothing new under the sun" (Ecclesiastes 1:9). Those who are unfamiliar with history are doomed to repeat it.

For those reasons, now that we are beginning to become

familiar with the three-headed monster, I want to review its development in the next chapter. My own experience tells me the only way we can recognize and categorize the error that binds those we encounter is to be thoroughly familiar with the basics.

That came home to me graphically recently when I received a call from a Mormon elder's quorum president who said he had read one of my books. He said he had questions about his faith. Had I not known what to ask I might have treated the whole conversation as an opportunity to explain to him the deficiencies of Mormonism. That would have been a mistake, for his biggest problem was not Mormonism; it was secularism! I asked him what he thought about Jesus Christ.

"I'm very confused. I really don't know."

"Well, what do you know about God?"

"I don't even know if He exists," the man replied.

Now that is an amazing piece of information! I was glad I had not plunged ahead into a discussion of Mormonism. Remember: "Those who come to God must believe that He is and that He is a rewarder of those who diligently seek Him." Anyone who does not believe in God is a secularist. So I asked him if he was an evolutionist.

"Absolutely," he replied. "I teach high school physics." I knew I was on the right track. I began a dialogue with him about evolution.

In order to fix these challenging concepts in your mind, the next chapter will give you an overview of the history of the progress of evil philosophy.

6
The Roots of Error

In order to witness to hard cases it is necessary to understand their most basic philosophical *problems*. To do that we must possess a rudimentary understanding of the development of philosophical truth and error. If we understand where secularists, cultists and occultists depart from the Bible's revelation of God, man and salvation, we can better understand how to help them back to truth. The historical overviews you will read in this and the next chapter are a distillation of two years of research with as many as a hundred books on the development of the great philosophies and ideas of humanity. My goal was to untangle the roots of these philosophies from the historical belief in God and His Son.

Genesis is the book of beginnings. It paints the history of man in broad strokes: the creation, the Fall, the flood and the dispersion of humankind from the Tower of Babel. Genesis introduces us to the first great civilizations: the Babylonians, the Assyrians, the Egyptians.

Although anthropologists like to speculate about origins of human history in terms of hundreds of thousands or even millions of years, concrete evidence for human history, as we shall see, reaches barely past 4000 B.C. The solid historical/ archaeological record begins then, in the Middle East (what we referred to in elementary school as the Fertile Crescent). The earliest civilizations developed along the Tigris and Euphrates Rivers in Mesopotamia (Babylon) and along the Nile in Egypt. (Genesis 2:14 identifies the Tigris as one of the four tributaries of the river in the Garden of Eden.)

For the Christian, it is not really important to know when God created the earth. The secularist, however, *must* have an earth that is billions of years old. To account for the presence of mankind and culture through evolution, the secularist must have man developing from lower primates for hundreds of thousands or millions of years. In other words, a Christian could live with a human history of more than 6,000 years, but a secularist cannot live with a human history of fewer than hundreds of thousands of years. If the historical record indicates very ancient human history, the Christian is not threatened. If, however, archaeological evidence supports the abrupt appearance of humankind on the face of the earth rather recently, the secularist is in deep philosophical trouble.

The Bible teaches that man was scattered abroad over the face of the earth after the building of the Tower of Babel (Genesis 11:8). When the Bible records Jewish history beginning with Abraham at about 2500–2000 B.C., it coincides with the best archaeological evidence.

Jews and Christians mark the building of the tower at Babylon as the first event of significance following God's destruction of mankind by the flood. The construction of the tower was a religious event. The Bible quotes the builders of the tower as saying: "Come, let us build ourselves a city, and a tower whose top is in the heavens; let us make a name for ourselves" (Genesis 11:4).

Archaeology confirms that the Babylonian towers (ziggu-rats) were religious temples designed to allow man to access heaven. According to the NIV Study Bible (referencing Genesis 11:4):

> The people's plans were egotistical and proud. . . . The typical Mesopotamian temple-tower, known as a ziggurat, was square at the base and had sloping, stepped sides that led upward to a small shrine at the top. . . . Ziggurats were given names demonstrating that they, too, were meant to serve as staircases from earth to heaven: "The House of the Link between Heaven and Earth" (at Larsa), "The House of the Seven Guides of Heaven and Earth" (at Borsippa), "The House of the Foundation-Platform of Heaven and Earth" (at Babylon), "The House of the Mountain of the Universe" (at Asshur).

Babylon, in the Bible, is symbolic not only of the enemies of God, but of witchcraft and evil, as we have already seen. In the Old Testament, Babylon is Israel's bane and oppressor, mentioned more than 150 times. In the New Testament, the book of Revelation speaks of the final judgments of God upon evil in the earth: "Babylon is fallen . . . because she has made all nations drink of the wine of the wrath of her fornication" (Revelation 14:8). The name of the scarlet woman on the scarlet beast in Revelation 17 is

MYSTERY,

BABYLON THE GREAT,

THE MOTHER OF HARLOTS

AND OF THE ABOMINATIONS

OF THE EARTH.

> I saw the woman, drunk with the blood of the saints
> and with the blood of the martyrs of Jesus. And . . . I
> marveled with great amazement.   Revelation 17:5–6

God identifies the spirit of the building of the Tower of Babel as religious rebellion. As such, it symbolizes rebellion against God's redemptive plan for mankind. It is man striving to do what only God can do—bridge the gap between sinful man and sinless God.

The self-righteous religious impulse is basic to the battle between the devil and God. Man, seeing his separation from God, does not humbly seek peace, but rebelliously storms heaven. This concept reveals man's basic fallen, prideful nature, a reiteration of the same rebellion Satan initiated in the Garden of Eden.

After the building of the Tower of Babel, God confused the language of mankind and dispersed the people throughout the earth. Sometime later God revealed Himself to Abraham, establishing contact that would remain unbroken through Judeo-Christian history. As we have noted, the devil has never ceased his attempts to thwart, block or hinder the revelation of God. Babylonian thinking spread from the Tower site to Egypt in the south and India in the west. The devil continued to attempt to sell mankind on the idea that he could become God, a god or equal to God. All false religion—all paganism, witchcraft and New Age thinking—is based on this concept.

As we examine the world's great philosophical ideas in the light of the biblical revelation, we see the satanic marks throughout history.

Western Paganism

Not long after God revealed Himself to Abraham, paganism was being formulated in Greece. By 1500 B.C. the Mycenaean Greeks succumbed to the invasion of "sea peoples." (Troy fell in 1230.) The sea peoples, the "Philistines," also conquered the east coast of the Mediterranean and threatened Egypt.

By 750 B.C. alphabetic writing was common in Greece; the first Olympic games were being held; philosophy and homosexuality occupied the men at the gymnasiums; and Greek gods were worshiped in glen and temple. (Divination reached a high religious form with the oracles of Delphi.)

By 400 B.C. (Socrates was executed in 399) philosophy reached its zenith in Greece. Philosophers had decided a hundred years earlier that a Creator existed at the foundation of the universe. Plato was a student of Socrates, Aristotle a student of Plato. Platonism became one of the most powerful philosophies ever devised and is still strong today.

Plato promoted the idea of Creator. He reasoned that nothing moves in the universe that has not first been moved by something else. He called that "First Mover" God.

Plato also believed in a human soul that survives death. He extended that belief into transmigration—reincarnation. Basically, for Plato, the material world was a projection of a perfect spiritual world. Flesh was only a poor reflection of reality, which was spirit. Man's task was to move out of the realm of the flesh and into the realm of the spirit by escaping the flesh through asceticism and the pursuit of beauty and philosophical truth. In 200 A.D., Plotinus adapted Plato's ideas and began the school we call Neoplatonism.

Neoplatonism became a broad, complex philosophical-theological system of many schools. It describes levels of existence separating man from God and seeks to develop a methodology by which man can return to God—or, rather, ways by which man can ascend from flesh to spirit. Neoplatonism is nothing more than a philosophical Tower of Babel.

Eastern Paganism

The Indus River Valley was settled in 1500 B.C. by nomadic tribes from the north. Like Greek paganism, the religion of these tribes, which came to be known as Hinduism, is polytheistic. Hindu philosophy (again like Platonism) teaches reincarnation, that the human soul returns to earth repeatedly in a cycle of death and rebirth. Hinduism teaches that man makes his way to oneness with God through good works, meditation or other religious acts. Again, it is a religious system whereby the individual can ascend to God.

The Good News

In contrast to the religious deception of the devil stands the revelation of God's message—the Good News. The Gospel message declares there is a simple solution to the sin of mankind. It is a solution supplied by a righteous God through the element of simple faith. It stands in opposition to all previous or subsequent philosophical and religious thought. The way to God is not through man's striving, but through God's work. Man's job is to acknowledge his inability to save himself and to submit himself humbly to God's provision of salvation.

All other systems are but the devil's old wine in new bottles. The deception is the same; the answer is the same. The job of hard case witnessing is to identify that facet of the old lie that today, in new dress, most separates our unsaved brothers and sisters from God, then take action against that lie by applying truth to it.

The next chapter, the final in this section on understanding hard cases, looks at the rise of secularism in the Western world. The third section of this book contains six chapters, two each on all three main categories—secularism, occultism and cultism—and will teach strategies for confronting them. Since secularism is by far the broadest, most fundamental and deep-rooted philosophy challenging us in the Western world, we will take it up first.

The secularization of America, in fact, is responsible for the rise of the occult and the cults. In the absence of the light of the Gospel, it is the poverty of secularism that has allowed the cults to take root and grow. It is the emptiness of secularism that has cleared the way for the Eastern mystical movement to sweep over our nation.

7
The New Dark Ages

Serious atheism—secularism—developed only within the last three hundred years. Although skepticism (the idea that we can never know anything with certainty) was a minority philosophical position in ancient Greek thought, atheism had never done well. Mankind is insistently religious. Even though Greek philosophers—the founders of Western civilization—espoused anti-biblical ideas, such as reincarnation, they did, as I mentioned earlier, believe from observing the universe that a Superintellect existed behind creation. Socrates, Plato and Aristotle, in seeking a perfect world, laid a philosophical foundation for theism—the belief in God.

This search for a Being greater than themselves is not surprising in light of Scripture. The Bible states plainly that God instills in every person an innate sense of His existence. This basic revelation of God is called "general revelation" and it is made known to us through the glory of God's creation: "Since the creation of the world His invisible attributes are clearly seen, being understood by the things that are made, even His eternal power and Godhead" (Romans 1:20).

The revelation of God in creation caused David to write these words a thousand years before Christ:

> The heavens declare the glory of
>   God;
> And the firmament shows His
>   handiwork.
> Day unto day utters speech,
> And night unto night reveals
>   knowledge.
> There is no speech nor
>   language
> Where their voice is not heard.
> Their line has gone out
>   through all the earth,
> And their words to the end of the world.
>
> Psalm 19:1–4

Because of the innate knowledge of God, the Bible declares that only a "fool has said in his heart, 'There is no God' " (Psalm 14:1). How is it, then, that mankind misses God? The answer is found in the rebellious nature of humanity. People choose idolatry and sin—adultery, fornication, homosexuality and murder—rather than submission to God (see Romans 1:21–32). They reject the knowledge of God because if God exists, they must be subject to Him!

But even as they ask questions, they (and we) are biased investigators. Everyone is bent away from godliness: "The heart is deceitful above all things, and desperately wicked; who can know it?" (Jeremiah 17:9). Couple mankind's inherited rebellion against God with the devil's strategy of lies, and you can understand why alternatives to the revelation of His nature continue to endure.

Today we live in a world in which atheism is everywhere prevalent. The entire superstructure of Communist thinking rests on dialectical materialism, the atheistic philosophy of Marx and Lenin. Western Europe is solidly secular, declaring a mechanical universe. Most of the American academic world and educational system is secular.

Still, the belief in God was thoroughly entrenched in the Western mind; we did not arrive at secularism easily. How have we come to have millions of atheists—secularists—in the world today? To understand the process, it is necessary to review the development of atheism over the last few centuries.

The Roots of Secularism

Three forces combined to provide man with an escape from God: the end of the authoritarianism of the Dark Ages, the rise of humanism and the growth of science.

During the centuries before and after the birth of Christ, Rome built its Empire upon the civilization of Greece. Its unified government established trade and communication throughout the expanding Empire, and allowed ideas, including Christianity, to spread rapidly. By the fifth century A.D., just before the fall of Rome, Christianity had become the state Roman religion and had spread throughout the Western world.

When the Empire fell to the invading Huns, the government collapsed and the part of the Empire we know as Europe was plunged into the Dark Ages. For a thousand years Europe was a mire of bloody conflict as serfdoms struggled with neighboring principalities in a maze of war, assassination, alliance, disease, poverty and ignorance.

The Roman Catholic Church preserved the little memory of government and philosophy that was not lost to the barbaric hordes. The teachings of philosophy and science were encapsulated in the libraries and disciplines of the monasteries. In time, the Church succumbed to the barbaric influences of the conquering pagan warriors, as paganism found its way into many practices of the Church.

The Renaissance was born in the wake of the Black Death, which swept Europe in the mid-fourteenth century; between 1348 and 1377 some forty percent of the global population was lost. With the end of the Plague, the government began to stabilize and international trade began to emerge. With trade, communication and a degree of sanity in government, the Greek masters were rediscovered; the Renaissance blossomed.

This rekindling of government and learning began to improve the lot of mankind. Optimism replaced fatalism and an emphasis on the dignity and worth of humanity emerged; man had potential for a good life now, not simply in the hereafter.

The stage was set for humanism, which at heart dignified individuals against the "divine right" authoritarianism of Church and state. It is important to note that humanism was not, in itself, contradictory to Christianity. Many of the great lights of the Protestant Reformation were humanists, trying to reject the dominance of the corrupt Church with the light of knowledge preserved from Greek antiquity. The Renaissance allowed the authority of the Church to be challenged by leaders of the Protestant Reformation—men like John Wycliffe, Martin Luther and Ulrich Zwingli.

By 1500 A.D., England had evolved from a coarse, brutal

feudalism (eight of the eighteen kings who ruled England between 1066 and 1485 died violent deaths) into a parliamentary government. Henry VIII broke with the Roman Catholic Church in 1534. The last heretic was burned in England in 1610 and the Puritan Revolution sent the Pilgrim fathers to America in 1620. The air of religious freedom caused the English parliamentary society to question how far the reformation of the Church should be allowed to go. They decided there could be no limits.

Interestingly, many of the emerging great scientists were deeply religious: Galileo, Robert Boyle and, perhaps the greatest of all, Sir Isaac Newton. (According to one historical account, at the end of his life Newton spent more time studying and writing about the Bible than he did science.)

It was Newton, ironically, who laid the foundational science that would be used to undergird the secularism of today. Newton's *Principia Mathematica* (1687) described the laws of motion and a clockwork universe. For Newton, the universe was evidence for a Creator God. Unfortunately, others used Newton's theories to describe the universe as a machine that could get along without God.

The seventeenth century became known as the Age of Reason; the eighteenth, the Enlightenment, as scientists struggled to understand the new universe that appeared in their microscopes and telescopes. Suddenly the world was infinitely more complex and wonderful than anyone had imagined. Copernicus revealed that the earth was not the center of the universe. People began to question the biblical account of creation. Could there be another explanation for the universe? If the Bible should prove to be wrong about the material world, could it be wrong about the very nature of God?

It is important to realize that much of what medieval man *thought* the Bible taught about the universe was not what the Bible taught at all. Rather, it was what the existing Church mistakenly understood the Bible to teach. When Galileo came into conflict with the Roman Catholic Church, he was not in conflict with the Bible, but with erroneous dogmatic concepts that the Church embraced.

The Church, in other words, had used the Bible to validate faulty medieval science. It now found itself dogmatically connected to an incomplete science and unable to let go. Many of the new scientists rejected not what the Bible declared, but what the Church declared. That subtle distinction was, however, often unrecognized in what was shaping up to be a battle between science and God.

The first step toward modern atheism was to shake the knowledge of the biblical God as Creator and sustainer of life, and as moral lawgiver. As humanism dignified (and often idealized) man, it led some to ask if they could not find God without the constraints of Christian dogma. Their concept of the "noble savage" sketched aboriginal man as the possessor of a "natural religion" that allowed him to worship God rightly without a Bible or other specific revelation from God. This line of thinking led to deism, which excludes God from the workings of the universe.

Science convinced deists that the universe was a machine. But a machine could not create itself: There had to be a Creator—the First Cause. The universe worked so well and by such divinely established laws that they decided God, who was necessary to create it, was just as unnecessary to maintain it. The universe worked too well; God had become super-fluous! God became the "Supreme Mechanic," the "Divine Watchmaker." People began to look within themselves for a sense of morality.

Men like John Locke of England, Voltaire of France and Thomas Jefferson of America were prominent deists. They labored for peace, justice and morality, while scorning the revealed religion of Christianity. Voltaire was the most violent in his opposition, saying of the Christian Church, "Crush the infamous thing!" Revealed religion—the religion of the Old and New Testaments—was seen as the antithesis to the God of reason and enlightenment.

Deism failed because it was a compromise position. The deists, abandoning revelation, eventually had to choose between secularism or occultism.

The move to full secularism is seen in David Hume, the Scottish historian and philosopher who wrote *Essay on Miracles* in 1748. Hume and others began to build a platform of literature for secularism. To do so, they needed to confront the arguments of Christianity. They needed an alternative to the Christian explanation not only for the complexity and beauty of the universe, but also for the emotional and artistic nature of the human mind. They struggled with this theory of mind—today called psychology. Alongside their version of the Newtonian "world machine," they developed its equivalent: the human mind machine.

What enlightened intellectuals lacked was a unified theory that could account for the wonder and complexity of the human mind and body without God. How could material forces alone account for all the wonders of the universe? How could they explain the universe, including animal and human life, without God?

These questions were answered for them in 1859 by Charles Darwin. His theory about evolution left an incalculable impact on Western culture. We will continue with the secularists' strong reliance on evolution and begin to see how to combat it in the next chapter.

Section 3
Confronting Hard
Cases

8
The Idol of Secularism: Evolution

Imagine a primitive tribe standing on a beach, clustered around a huge crate that has washed up on the shore. As they pull away the boards and rip open the plastic packing, they uncover a beautiful mahogany clock. They are awestruck as each hour it emits melodic gongs from within its breast.

The people speculate as to its meaning. After a while they begin to observe a pattern to the sounding gongs: When the sun stands precisely overhead it sounds twelve gongs; then after one of the two sticks on its face moves in a complete circle it sounds one gong, and, after another revolution, two gongs. This continues until it again sounds twelve gongs in the middle of the night. This pattern repeats itself day and night.

As time passes their reactions become matter-of-fact. The women of the village begin to prepare morning and evening meals when the sticks are straight up and down. Eventually, the elders declare the device a gift from God. That viewpoint is believed because no other explanation seems possible.

One day, however, one of the elders says he doesn't believe

the device came from God. He advances the theory that natural forces on a distant island shaped it. The wood was sculpted by fire and water and wind. The shiny parts were formed by lightning and heat. Somehow the entire project was completed by natural accident. The tribe, he says, is a recipient not of a gift from God, but of a happy accident. And this theory begins to prevail.

That scenario represents the development of the theory of evolution. The generally accepted belief in God held until the eighteenth-century Enlightenment, when elders of science announced that they no longer believed life was a creation of God. It was but a cosmic accident. This was a new and radical idea, and it challenged the philosophical consensus of human history.

Great social pressure challenged the old ways, particularly explanations of the creation of the world as described in the Bible. As we saw at the end of chapter 7, what the new rebels lacked was a unified theory to undergird their rising impatience with Bible revelation.

Darwin

The main problem facing the Enlightenment thinkers was the origin of all the different species of life: How can we account for the profusion of life forms without God? Various individuals advanced theories suggesting that the similarities among the species indicated everything arose from one primary life form. That idea was considered for at least a hundred years before Darwin set forth his theory.

The French philosopher Denis Diderot suggested in 1753 that "there never was more than one primeval animal, the prototype of all." Darwin's grandfather, Erasmus Darwin, was a convinced evolutionist by 1794, but he too lacked a theory to describe what he wanted to believe. Another naturalist, Chevalier de Lamrack, sorted animals into an evolutionary tree from microanimals to man. He proposed that new species emerged because organisms desired certain changes to take place. He called this motivational force "natural sentiment."

Charles Darwin called his theory "natural selection." He suggested that the environment created pressures that allowed those individuals best adapted to survive. Natural selection has commonly been called survival of the fittest. In one famous example Darwin postulated that giraffes had developed long necks because drought reduced the availability of food. The long-necked giraffes were able to eat leaves at the tops of the trees which were inaccessible to other animals. Short-necked giraffes died out. (No short-necked giraffe fossils have ever been discovered.)

In 1859 Darwin published *On the Origin of Species* to account for the proliferation of life forms through natural selection. The impact of that book is unequaled in secular human history. The implications of Darwinism are with us today in every scientific field, including biology, geology, astronomy and sociology. Objective investigators should remember that the initial battle was more philosophical than scientific. The question being asked was, "Where did we come from?" Evolution's answer differed from history's, which was, "We are here because God created us."

The furious debate occasioned by *On the Origin of Species* continues today. Evolutionists line up against creationists. Court cases test whether or not creationism can be taught alongside evolution in the classroom.

Christian Evolutionists?

I believe it is possible to be a Christian evolutionist. God does not require, as a prerequisite to salvation, that a person be able to understand how He brought the universe into existence. Many people believe God created the universe using the natural process we call evolution. These are theistic evolutionists, as opposed to atheistic evolutionists of the Marx/Lenin type.

Theistic evolutionists ask, "Couldn't God have created the beginnings of life and then let it evolve into its present complexity and profusion?" The answer is, Of course. Yes, He could have done so. But did He?

We need to answer that question because millions of secularists rely on the theory of evolution as their primary defense for atheism. It is impossible to be a solid secularist if evolution has not occurred. Those who, like Isaac Asimov, believe there is no spiritual dimension must have the theory of evolution: Without it no rational explanation can account for mankind's existence except special creation by God.

If evolution is not true—and if we can demonstrate that—the secularist may be motivated to reconsider the existence of God.

Our Secular Society

Secularism is caught in an endless cycle of circular reasoning. Human beings asked the question, "How could man exist if there were no God?" The theory of evolution was proposed to answer the question. Then came the question, "How do we know there is no God?" And the answer, "Because man was formed through evolution."

Evolution is now the *a priori* explanation for what we observe in nature. For example: Evolution says complex life forms evolved from lower life forms. So, we date rock formations by the fossils contained in them. When we want to date those fossils, on the other hand, we date them by the rock formations they were found in. This kind of circular reasoning is called a tautology. (We will talk more about fossils in chapter 9.)

Today most children are taught evolution in school as though it were established fact. Academia believes, by and large, that evolution is science and special creation is "merely" religion. Some scientists take very anti-creationist positions. Ernst Mayr, the ornithologist who redefined biology's concept of the term *species*, is one such scientist. Mayr determined that species should not be classified according to how they look, but rather by their ability to interbreed. The earmark of a true species is reproductive distinctiveness: One species cannot breed with another species to produce fertile offspring. As professor emeritus of zoology at Harvard, Mayr, in the science magazine *Omni*, blamed Christianity not only for the "intellectual stagnation of the Dark Ages," but for the "nonsense" of wanting to introduce teachings of the Bible into classrooms on equal footing with "established scientific fact," by which he meant evolution.

Likewise, Harvard paleontologist Stephen Jay Gould, writing in May 1981 in the science magazine *Discover*, was both "angry at and amused by the Creationists." But mostly he was "deeply sad . . . because Evolution is one of the half dozen 'great ideas' developed by science." Carl Sagan, dean of the secular community, writing as president of The Planetary Society in 1985, sent out a mailing in which he said America's exploration of space was "as significant as our ancestors' descent from the trees."

In view of those kinds of statements from our foremost scientists, it is little wonder the average Christian is uneasy when evangelicals speak openly of evolution as anything less than good science. But is the belief in evolution based on an objective evaluation of scientific data, or is evolution itself a religious belief system?

While the majority of scientists believe in evolution, thousands do not. Many eminent scientists agree with Dr. Robert Gange, an award-winning NASA research scientist, who calls evolution "the secret and irrational worship of interstellar dust under the guise of atheism." World famous philosopher/scientist Karl Popper spoke for many scientists when he said evolution does not even qualify as a legitimate scientific theory because it can never be finally proven nor disproven. Dr. Colin Patterson, senior paleontologist and editor of a prestigious journal at the British Museum of Natural History, has said there is no real evidence of evolutionary transitions either among living or fossilized organisms.

When people ask for the hard objective evidence behind the scientific community's ongoing declaration of confidence in evolution, they often come away stunned. They find little good evidence defended with near religious fervor. Dr. Gange takes Popper's statements even further, calling the theory of evolution "not a scientific theory . . . [but rather] a conjectural apologetic for materialism."

My own personal experience of having my eyes opened to evolution is typical. In 1981 I took a vacation trip through Dinosaur National Monument in Utah. I was fascinated with the unearthing of the fossils of these magnificent beasts. A few days later at the Denver Museum of Natural History I was again awestruck by the size and reality of these ancient creatures. Like so many others, I assumed that the reality of extinct dinosaurs in some way vindicated evolution.

While this new sense of mystery hung in my memory I happened upon a book entitled *Evolution: The Fossils Say No!* I supposed the book was by a crackpot or amateur scientist and nearly passed it by when I turned it over to see that it was written by a man with an earned doctorate in biology from the University of California, Berkeley, Dr. Duane Gish.

As we headed home from our vacation, driving through two days of cloudbursts across the red desert of southern Wyoming, my wife read the book to me. I was astonished by page after page of evidence that indicated the fossil record does not bear out the theory of evolution. I swore I would study the matter for myself. Remember, I had no ax to grind. My theology was not threatened by evolution. I could be a Christian whether or not evolution was true. But, as I discovered and have indicated here, evolutionists have a vested interest in evolution being true. If it is not true, their secularism is threatened.

I tell that story because it is typical. People who investigate evolution objectively are surprised by its tenuous foundation. I'll go further than that: The only people who cling to it after a serious investigation are those who—for whatever reason—cannot bring themselves to consider special creation by God as an explanation for the universe and the origin of species. The fact is that evolution continues to be considered seriously by intelligent people (after objective investigation) only if they are threatened by the alternative—special creation of the universe by God. Over and over again you will discover evolutionists saying something like, "Whatever the problems with evolution, the alternative is impossible." As Dr. Gange says, evolutionists pursue their cause with religious zeal and evaluate it by standards far less stringent than those they use to evaluate all other scientific matters.

Foundation of Evolution

Dr. George Wald is typical of those openly taking this stance. Wald, who won the Nobel Prize in 1967 for his work in identifying the chemical process by which the retina differentiates colors of light, once wrote an article in *Scientific American* (Vol. 191) entitled "The Origin of Life":

> About a century ago the question, How did life begin? which has interested men throughout their history, reached an impasse. Up to that time two answers had been offered: one that life had been created supernaturally, the other that it arises continually from the nonliving. The first explanation lay outside science; the second was now shown to be untenable.

Wald goes on to say that the debate over life arising from nonlife—spontaneous generation—had been demonstrated to be an impossibility by men like Francesco Redi, Lazzaro Spallanzani and, finally, Louis Pasteur. These men demonstrated scientifically the error of those who believed worms arose spontaneously out of mud, or maggots from decaying meat. Pasteur, Wald said, forever settled the issue.

The argument stemmed from the fact that nutritive broth, which forms mold under normal circumstances, was shown by Spallanzani not to do so if it were boiled and then sealed while boiling (this was the beginning of modern food preservation—canning). Spallanzani said this proved that the microorganisms that made up the mold did not come into being spontaneously, but were introduced to the broth through impurities in the air. His detractors argued that mold did not form because his process excluded air, which was a crucial component of the mix.

Pasteur then took up the experiment by placing broth in a bottle with a long S-shaped neck, which allowed air to get to the broth but prohibited dust—and thus microorganisms—from getting to the broth. No mold formed. Wald says that when Pasteur finished his experiments, "nothing remained of the belief in spontaneous generation."

Wald says that faced with the two options—spontaneous generation or an act of supernatural creation—a scientist who chooses *not* to believe in an act of God has no choice but to accept spontaneous generation as the explanation for life. Why? Because the idea of creation lies outside of science, and these scientists have no other alternative—thus they choose to believe something that could not happen. This is irrational for a scientist, but such are the mental gymnastics of those who choose not to believe in God.

How It Works

Today, a beginning biology student will be taught that spontaneous generation was demonstrated by Pasteur to be impossible. In fact, in the opening chapters of a Biology 101 textbook, the concept of biogenesis will be taught: Biogenesis states that life can come only from other life. But somewhere around chapter four, the student is told that evolution must be assumed to be true. For the rest of the student's biological education, that assumption is made.

The same circular reasoning exists wherever evolution is

taught. The theory is so much a part of our everyday life that no amount of proof will do it in. Dr. Paul Ehrlich, the famous biologist of the original Earth Day fame, says in an article in *Nature* (Vol. 214): "No one can think of ways to test [evolution]. Ideas, either without basis or based on a few laboratory experiments carried out in extremely simplified systems, have attained currency far beyond their validity."

One of the world's most eminent astronomers, Sir Fred Hoyle, says the chance that life may have emerged through biological evolution in our solar system is impossible. There simply is not enough time for that to have occurred, even if the earth is 4.7 billion years old. Hoyle says it is as likely as "a tornado sweeping through a junk-yard [and assembling] a Boeing 747 from the materials therein" (*Nature*, Vol. 294). Hoyle continues to be an evolutionist, but he thinks evolution must have happened somewhere else. Some suggest that life evolved outside our solar system and either arrived on a meteorite or was sent by intelligent life from another solar system.

How Can We Proceed?

The key to reaching secularists is in the rational presentation of arguments against the idol of evolution. In the next chapter we will take a look at the arguments of evolutionists and present the evidence with which those arguments are refuted.

People do change their minds about evolution, as evidenced in the interesting change of thinking by Dr. Colin Patterson, senior paleontologist at the British Museum of Natural History. In his keynote address at the American Museum of Natural History in 1981 he said:

One morning I woke up and . . . it struck me that I had been working on [evolution] for twenty years and there was not one thing I knew about it. That's quite a shock to learn that one can be so misled so long. Either there was something wrong with me or there was something wrong with evolutionary theory. Naturally, I know there is nothing wrong with me, so for the last few weeks I've tried putting a simple question to various people and groups of people.

Question is, "Can you tell me anything you know about evolution, any one thing, any one thing that is true?" I tried that question on the geology staff at the Field Museum of Natural History and the only answer I got was silence. I tried it on the members of the Evolutionary Morphology Seminar at the University of Chicago, a very prestigious body of evolutionists, and all I got there was silence for a long time and eventually one person said, "I do know one thing—it ought not be taught in high school."

9
Confronting Secularism

Fifteen billion years ago, the secularist believes, all the matter in the universe was condensed into a microscopically small point in space before it exploded in what astronomers call the Big Bang. As the exploding matter traveled outward, it began to arrange itself, through *chance*, into combinations of ever-increasing complexity. All the stars and galaxies were formed by this process. The sun and earth were formed about five billion years ago.

Eventually this same process created life on the earth as inorganic substances in the atmosphere—hydrogen, water, ammonia and methane—were subjected to ultraviolet light and lightning. Chance processes then formed large numbers of *organic* compounds like fatty and amino acids, until finally a living cell evolved spontaneously from a watery soup of these compounds.

Evolutionary theory goes on to say that all life forms—from the simplest one-celled organisms to plants, butterflies, rhinoceroses and men—were derived from the random movement of matter. Cosmic dust in motion, evolution says, arranged itself in ever-increasing complexity without the benefit of God.

Surprisingly, the theories astrophysicists advance for this origin of the universe are based on scanty evidence. They are highly speculative and subject to dramatic revision with each new discovery of science. Now, radically different theories regularly replace old ones. In light of the frequency at which one theory is replaced by another, it is a wonder that the new theories are embraced with so much enthusiasm and conviction.

The Big Bang Theory

The Big Bang theory just referred to, for example, is of very recent origin. Until 1929 science taught unanimously what was called the "steady state" theory of the universe: The universe has existed forever much as it now is. This theory was, at least, in harmony with the First Law of Thermodynamics, which says nothing can come into being through natural processes: No new matter can be created.

In 1924, however, Edwin Hubble detected what is called the red-shift effect of starlight, which allowed him, in 1929, to conclude that all the galaxies are traveling away from each other. He decided the galaxies must be moving outward from a common point in the universe. Scientists, therefore, postulated a time when the universe came into being—a *creation*. This was a radically new concept that instantly replaced hundreds of years of dedication to the steady state model. Since science rejected a supernatural Creator, the Big Bang theory was advanced in an attempt to explain a universe coming into being without God.

The Big Bang really solves nothing. It does not account for the creation of matter, it simply starts with a microdot of infinitely compressed matter. But where did the matter come from? Advocates of the Big Bang theory say that question is irrelevant: Whatever occurred before the Big Bang is unknowable and, therefore, simply not important to those of us who exist on this side of that moment.

It is worth noting that secularists who scoff at the Christian's faith in God are themselves believers. They wonder at the Christian's ability to believe in a supernatural Being who created cosmic dust or "matter." "Where did *He* come from?" they ask. "How can you believe in a God who just is?" At the same time, they themselves believe in dust, content that it just is. Both Christians and secularists exercise faith: One exercises faith in God, who is self-existent; the other exercises faith in dust itself, which just exists. It is not a question of *who* is a believer, it's only a question of *what* we choose to believe in.

It is of further interest to note that the eminent astrophysicist Stephen Hawking suggests in his book *A Brief History of Time* (p. 42) that Hubble's discovery of receding galaxies creates an interesting dilemma for astronomers. Hubble, Hawking says, only proves that galaxies are moving away *from the earth*. At first glance, he says, we might conclude that our own solar system is at the center of the universe, with everything moving away from it. (This is an interesting speculation since the Genesis account places the creation of the earth on the first day and the stars on the fourth day.) Hawking says there is no good reason to suppose we are *not* at the center of the universe, but we tend not to want to. The only reason we *don't* believe that, he says, is modesty: We simply cannot believe we are important enough to be at the center of things.

The Big Bang theorizes that the amazingly complex atomic structure was born in the explosion. The precise relationships of protons, neutrons and electrons, which move and interreact according to fixed and predictable laws—all are the result of chance. Again, Hawking suggests it is mind-boggling that all these phenomenal things should happen. The odds against it are astronomical. How can we account for a universe organizing itself precisely to support a planet like ours with complex systems in place to support life? Perhaps, Hawking suggests, there are an infinite number of universes and we happen to be in the one that can support life.

Robert Gange calls theories of the evolution of inorganic chemical compounds "simply irrational." He then asks: "If we cannot conceive of a rational methodology by which simpler inorganic elements came into being through natural causes, how can we then conclude that living organisms—which are vastly more complex—came into existence through natural causes?"

French biologist Louis Bounoure called evolution a useless scientific theory, "a fairy tale for grown-ups" (*The Advocate*, March 8, 1984). Philosopher/journalist Malcolm Muggeridge once observed in a lecture at the University of Waterloo that "the theory of evolution . . . will be one of the great jokes of history books of the future."

The degree of self-deception that exists in the infrastructure of evolutionary theory is as phenomenal as the theory itself. *We must never lose sight of the fact that evolution is not a theory that arose from a preponderance of factual evidence; it is a theory advanced in an attempt to offer another explanation besides the well-established biblical one.* The evolution of the theory of evolution is the story of desperate searchers intent on finding bits and pieces of evidence for their preconceived notion of a universe without God.

Nevertheless, proponents of evolution from the scientific community are a strong-minded lot and not prone to consider readily the alternative. *Scientific American,* for example, one of the nation's oldest and most prestigious science magazines, recently dropped a new monthly columnist who admitted (when asked) to being a creationist. Although editor Jonathan Piel described the work of Forrest Mims III, a veteran freelance science writer, as "first-rate," he expressed concern that the "good name of the magazine" might be "embarrassed." A former editor with *Scientific American,* Tim Appenzeller (now a senior editor at *The Sciences*), confirmed that Mims was dropped because of his beliefs about evolution and his rejection of Darwinian selection.

Subjects of Importance

How then shall we approach our secularist friends through a discussion of evolution? First, they will need to be confronted with the fact that evolution is an inadequate explanation for the origin of life. Our hope is that when reasonable people are presented with truth they often change their own preconceptions. We hope they will open themselves up to the truth that the God who created them also loves them and desires to redeem them. To challenge their secular philosophy, I offer the following ten arguments against evolution.

One: The Fossil Record

The most convincing proof is in the fossil record itself. Darwin noticed that variations occurred in the offspring of a species as environmental conditions changed. Those offspring survived that were the best adapted. But Darwin took a major and untenable leap, assuming that these adaptations eventually created new species. The usual supposition, for example, is that fish developed into amphibians and reptiles. Then reptiles, through millions of minute adaptations, became birds—they developed wings and began to fly. Thus the evolutionary tree is drawn.

Such developments should be evidenced in the fossil record. There should be fossils from every stage in the development of a reptile into a bird, or a fish into an amphibian, or an ape into a man. *The fact is the fossil record shows no such progression.*

Evolutionists can produce only a fossil record that shows the immediate appearance of fully developed species— exactly what Christians who believe the Bible account of creation would expect. The fact that species appear instantly in the fossil record with no "transitional forms" is the evolutionist's nightmare. They are *themselves* amazed that transitional fossil forms do not exist. It is a mystery to them. They reason, since evolution is true, that transitional forms *must* exist. But they don't!

We should, for instance, have fossil records that show a reptile beginning to develop wings. We should be able to line up thousands of fossils displaying minute changes in the structure of the developing wings. We can't do that. No such fossils exist. Evolutionists and non-evolutionists alike agree on that.

This obvious defect in the fossil record was observed by Darwin himself. In *On the Origin of Species* (pp. 292–293) he asked the question,

> Why then is not every geological formation and every stratum full of such intermediate links? Geology assuredly does not reveal any such finely graduated organic chain; and this, perhaps, is the most obvious and serious objection which can be urged against the theory.

Modern scientists seem forced to concur: Eminent paleontologist Stephen Jay Gould of Harvard University says we cannot construct "even in our imagination" a fossil chain for evidence for intermediary stages (*Paleobiology*, Vol. 6 [1]). David B. Kitts, writing in the scientific journal *Evolution* (Vol. 28), said, "Evolution requires intermediate forms between species and *paleontology does not provide them*" (emphasis added).

Two: The Horse Series

The lack of transitional forms forced biologists to speculate that Darwin was wrong. Still they continued with theories. One, the "horse series," is a famous example often taught in American schools. It supposedly depicts the evolution of the horse in North America from a small dog-sized animal. While there are fossils showing various sizes and shapes of the horse, there are no intermediate stages; the transitions are not smooth and continuous.

In the 1950s Swedish scientist Heribert Nilsson commented, "The family tree of the horse is beautiful and continuous only in the textbooks" (*Artbuldung, Verlag CWE Gleerup*). Other scientists have expressed similar misgivings about the gaps in the horse fossils. In 1952, for instance, Richard B. Goldschmidt, professor of genetics and cytology at the University of California, wrote in *American Scientist* (Vol. 40) that "within the slowly evolving series, like the famous horse series, the decisive steps are abrupt, without transition." In 1960 Professor G. A. Kerkut, a British biochemist, commented in his book *Implications of Evolution* (pp. 144–145), that "one could easily discuss the evolution of the *story* of the evolution of the horse" (emphasis added).

Goldschmidt, observing that the fossil record does not provide the evidence for Darwinism, decided new species must have appeared suddenly, jumping past the transitional forms. When he advanced this idea, his colleagues ridiculed him, saying it was laughable that one species gave birth to another radically different one. Someone tagged this idea "The Hopeful Monster Mechanism," suggesting it basically meant a reptile could lay an egg and a bird could hatch out of it.

Today, however, this same Hopeful Monster Mechanism—under a new name—is becoming the theory of choice among evolutionists. Scientist Stephen Jay Gould assesses the implications of the missing links: Darwinism simply cannot be true. Gould has postulated an updated theory he calls "Punctuated Equilibrium." Basically this theory says that species undergo relatively rapid and radical change in localized populations. In other words, a horse gained or lost toes or a reptile became a bird through a series of leaps that punctuated the equilibrium of relatively slow change.

Such a theory is, by definition, *not* a theory of evolution. The very word *evolution* implies a smooth, gradual change from one state into another. Punctuated Equilibrium attempts to make the fossil record compatible with the old theory. But the fact is, in the fossil record there is no evolution from one *species* to another.

Three: The Ape Series

That humans and apes evolved from a common ancestor is largely taken for granted today. We often see the familiar artist's portrayal of an ape turning into a man through a series of stages. But upon what evidence do we base this concept? We base it solely upon our predisposition to believe in evolution. If evolution is true, man *must* have evolved. Since apes have similar body structures to ours, evolutionists conclude they are our ancestors and set about to prove the connection. Nowhere is evidence more flimsy and contrived.

Is man evolving? Stephen Jay Gould thinks not. In a *Washington Times* article (Feb. 8, 1984) he said: "We're not just evolving slowly. For all practical purposes we're not evolving. There's no reason to think we're going to get bigger brains or smaller toes or whatever—we are what we are."

Sad to say, evolutionists often distort the evidence to fit their theory. The famous British anatomist Professor Lord Solly Zuckerman said: "Students of fossil primates have not been distinguished for [their] caution. . . . It is legitimate to ask whether much science is yet to be found in this field at all" (*Beyond the Ivory Tower*, p. 64).

And anthropologist Lyall Watson, writing in *Science Digest* (Vol. 90), said: "Modern apes . . . seem to have sprung out of nowhere. They have no yesterday, no fossil record. And the true origin of modern humans—of upright, naked, tool-making, big-brained beings—is . . . an equally mysterious matter."

Far too often anthropologists stretch the evidence to fit their preconceptions. Tim White, an anthropologist from the University of California, Berkeley, offers an explanation. He is quoted in an article in *New Scientist* (April 28, 1983) entitled "Hominid [early man] Collarbone Exposed As Dolphin's Rib": "The problem with a lot of anthropologists is that they want so much to find a hominid that any scrap of bone becomes a hominid bone."

The author of *Missing Links*, John Reader, said in *New Scientist:*

> The entire hominid collection known today would barely cover a billiard table. . . . The collection is so tantalizingly incomplete, and the specimens themselves often so fragmentary and inconclusive, that more can be said about what is missing than what is present. . . . Preconceptions have led evidence by the nose in the study of fossil man.

History bears out these preconceptions:

• The famous Nebraska man (Hesperopithecus), hawked by scientists as proof of evolution in the famous 1925 Scopes "Monkey Trial," was a specimen constructed in the minds of scientists from a single tooth! William Jennings Bryan, the lawyer who prosecuted the schoolteacher arrested for teaching evolution, was confronted by a battery of scientific experts who said the tooth proved man came from the apes. Bryan was left with little more argument than to stress that this was scanty evidence. He lost the case. Two years later, when the rest of the skeleton matching the tooth was excavated, paleontologists proved it to be not a hominid, but an extinct pig!

• The once-famous Java man was constructed of three teeth, part of a skull and a fragment of a thigh bone. Scientists concluded subsequently that there was no evidence the bones were part of the same creature. The original finder of the fragments, Dr. Eugene Dubois, eventually concluded the bones were the remains of some sort of gibbon.

• The Piltdown man, allegedly discovered in 1912 by Charles Dawson, fooled anthropologists for years. Piltdown Man was hailed in textbooks as proof of evolution until being exposed in 1953 as a hoax. Someone had filed down the teeth and discolored the bones and hidden them in a pit. Both

Dawson and his assistant at the time, the French priest Teilhard de Chardin, have been suggested as perpetrators of the scheme. Teilhard is suspected of desiring to harmonize evolution with Christianity.

• Neanderthal man was long touted as a link between man and ape. Today he is classified as *Homo sapiens*—fully human.

• The African "ancient man" fossils—the finds in the Olduvai River gorge in Africa by Louis and Mary Leakey—have led scientists to conclude man may be nearly two million years old. The fossils are far from conclusive.

One famous African fossil known as "Lucy" is used to date man at four million years. Lucy was discovered in Ethiopia by Donald Johanson. Lecturing at the University of Missouri in Kansas City on November 20, 1986, Johanson admitted parts of Lucy were found as far apart as two to three kilometers and separated by as much as 200 feet of rock strata. When asked why he was so sure the parts were from the same skeleton he replied, "Anatomical similarity."

Four: Evolution Is Never Observed

Besides the lack of fossil evidence for evolution, scientists were faced with the fact that evolution has never been observed directly. No new species has been developed in the laboratory or through animal husbandry or any other means.

That does not say, of course, that there is no variation *within* a species. We have a huge assortment of dogs—more than one hundred breeds from the giant mastiff to the Chihuahua—but all the variations fit within the gene structure of the dog species. We can have big dogs, little dogs, black dogs, white dogs, spotted dogs and all manner of variety within the predetermined gene spread. All these animals are dogs by anybody's classification. Cats (species *Felis catus*) cannot breed with dogs (*Canis familiaris*) to produce a new species. As the Bible says, life comes forth after its "kind." Likewise, human beings (*Homo sapiens*) come in assorted sizes, shapes and colors, from tall, Nordic types to pygmies, but they are all fully human.

It is also true that we can produce hybrids. In the Equus family, for example, a male donkey (*Equus asinus*) can breed with a mare (*Equus caballus*) and produce a mule. The mule is not a new species, however. Hybrids can be produced continually only by continuing to breed the original two species. They cannot reproduce themselves for more than one generation.

Advocates of evolution will sometimes point to variations within a species and attempt to call it evolution. The most famous examples are the dark and light forms of the peppered moth. Before the development of certain industrial areas, light-colored moths flourished because they were less visible than dark ones on the light bark of trees. Birds could see—and therefore eat—the dark ones. After factories produced pollutants that discolored the trees, the dark moths were less visible and, as a result, became more numerous in the population. At the same time the light moths began to disappear because they were more visible. But, according to L. Harrison Matthews, writing in the introduction to the 1971 edition of Darwin's *On the Origin of Species*, this does *not* show evolution in progress because the light and dark moths all continue to exist. One does not change into the other.

Five: Mutant Fruitflies

The driving force of evolution, Darwin said, was natural selection. But how did it work itself out in practical terms? As I said earlier, Lamrack had spoken of "natural sentiment," the idea that some innate force was driving species upward through the evolutionary chain. That sounded too much like a godlike creative power for the Darwinists. Operating without God, they needed some other motivating force. They came up with *chance*.

"Positive Chance Mutations" was the idea they supported. They decided that random gene mutations within an organism would produce "positive mutants," meaning mutations that were better adapted in some way than the ancestor. The problem with it is we have never been able to observe a positive mutation. Mutations are always deleterious (negative). A chromosome-damaged offspring is always less well adapted for life than the ancestor. Most mutations are, in fact, lethal.

In recent years scientists have attempted to bring about evolution in the laboratory through intentional gene mutation. They have, for example, irradiated millions of fruitflies over numerous generations. They have succeeded in producing blind flies, weak flies and flies with legs on their heads, but they have not produced flies that were either superior to their predecessors or new species. It is possible, of a certainty, to produce varieties within species by breeding, as noted above referring to mules. We can produce varieties of roses and tulips, but we are not producing new species, neither plant nor animal.

Six: The Quest for Time

While the dauntless evolutionists could not find evidence for the development of new species, they continued to postulate that all the millions of species evolved from one primordial ancestor. There was no evidence for transitional forms in the fossil record and, as time passed, it became obvious they were not going to observe the development of *new* species. Rather than abandon the theory of evolution, they said, "If we had enough time, we would see the evidence."

Thus began an insatiable quest for time. At first they felt they needed tens of thousands of years, but as their understanding of the complexity of life forms increased, they realized they needed still more time to observe the evolutionary process. The scientific estimation for the age of the earth has mushroomed for the last two hundred years until now we speak not of tens of thousands, or even tens of millions of years, but of *billions* of years. Today, as we have seen, even five billion years is not nearly enough.

Seven: Geological Dating

The upshot of the need for time is that evolutionists fell into a circular process for gaining time: They began to date the earth from the fossils found in the rocks. As the biological evolutionists set the clock back on the beginnings of life on earth, geological evolutionists recalibrated their rock strata!

The question is, "Which came first, the age of the rocks or the age of the fossils?" The fact is that for evolutionists fossils date the rocks and rocks date the fossils in the tautology we mentioned earlier. Thus, if we want to know the age of a particular rock stratum we look at the fossils in it and then date the rock by saying it contains twenty-million-year-old fossils. Then, when we find another fossil in that rock, we date that fossil at the age of the rock—twenty million years.

This kind of circular reasoning is questioned by many scientists. Niles Eldredge of the American Museum of Natural History wrote a book entitled *Time Frames: The Rethinking of Darwinian Evolution and the Theory of Punctuated Equilibria* (p. 52). In it he asks: "If we date the rocks by their fossils, how can we then turn around and talk about patterns of evolutionary change through time in the fossil record?" J. E. O'Rourke, writing in the *American Journal of Science* (Vol. 276), said:

> The intelligent layman has long suspected circular reasoning in the use of rocks to date fossils and fossils to date rocks. The geologist has never bothered to think of a good reply, feeling that explanations are not worth the trouble as long as the work brings results. This is supposed to be hard-headed pragmatism.

Another mistaken idea is that the fossils can be arranged in a sequential order in the rocks. We have all seen the diagrams—the geological time columns—showing the one-celled organisms in the deepest rock strata and increasingly complex fossils in the ascending strata. Is that the way it is, or is it wishful thinking?

In *Christianity Today* (September 14, 1962) Walter E. Lammerts said:

> The actual percentage of areas showing this progressive order from the simple to the complex is surprisingly small. Indeed formations with very complex forms of life are often found resting directly on the basic granites. Furthermore, I have in my own files a list of over 500 cases that attest to a reverse order, that is, simple forms of life resting on top of more advanced types.

The fact is there are massive graveyards around the world in which complex and simple life forms lie side by side. This testifies to a worldwide catastrophe, like the Genesis flood.

How is all this circular reasoning possible? *It is possible be-*

cause the geological time column is constructed upon the presumption of evolution. In his book *The Collapse of Evolution* (pp. 9–14) Scott Huse writes:

> Geologists during the 19th century began to compile the geologic column. They arranged the earth's strata according to the various types of fossils they contained, especially their index fossils (usually marine invertebrates which are easily recognized, assumed to have been widespread in occurrence, and of limited chronological duration) thus marking a specific age determination for a rock formation. Strata with similar fossils (presumed to have evolved first) were put on the bottom of the column while strata containing more complex forms (presumed to have evolved later) were placed toward the top of the column. Thus, the entire geologic column was founded and built on the assumption that organic evolution was a fact.

Eight: Dating the Age of the Earth

There are several ways scientists can try to determine the age of the earth. One way is through sedimentation rates—the rate at which rock strata form. The sedimentation rates are constantly being recalibrated. In the quest for more time, the sedimentation tables were recalibrated upward—during the years between 1900 and 1935, by a factor of 25,000 percent. The recalibration was based upon a new scientific discovery—radioactivity.

Radioactive Dating

Radioactive clocks are said to be extremely accurate. They are based on the principle that atomic structures emit particles within precise time constraints. By measuring the amount of radioactive decay that has occurred in a fossil, scientists think they can accurately determine the age of the fossil. The famous carbon-14 dating process is based on this principle.

Radioactive clocks are not the only chemical clocks. In fact, there are more than eighty ways in which the age of the earth may be estimated through the observation of natural processes. Of the eighty clocks, most of them teach much shorter earth ages than radioactive clocks. Only a handful show earth ages of billions of years.

The following examples of earth dating are accepted as general scientific knowledge and easily researched. They suggest a shorter earth duration than is usually realized.

• The sun's diameter is apparently shrinking by 8.3 miles every year. As recently as 1567 there was an eclipse of the sun in which the disc of the moon, as it passed between the earth and the sun, did not fully cover the disc of the sun as it does now. The fact of the shrinking sun places the age of the sun closer to tens of thousands of years.

• The earth's magnetic field also is shrinking rapidly. So fast, in fact, that if its rate is constant, the magnetic field of the earth forty thousand years ago would have been as strong as that of a neutron star, which scientists know to be impossible. Evolutionists are hoping to discover that the magnetic field pulsates, but no one can conceive of a way for that to occur. This observation also gives us an earth age of not more than a few tens of thousands of years.

• The earth is bombarded by fourteen million tons of meteoritic dust a year. If the earth were billions of years old, it should be covered with more than fifty feet of meteoritic dust.

Evolutionists argue that most of this dust is washed into the ocean. The content of meteoritic dust is rich in nickel but nickel is virtually nonexistent in ocean water. Likewise, the same collection rate is occurring on the moon. The moon has no water or oceans. It should be covered with a thick blanket of dust. So convinced were scientists that meteoritic dust has been accumulating at a uniform rate for millions of years that NASA designed the lunar lander with huge pods to keep it from sinking in the dust. They actually found a layer of dust only an eighth of an inch thick. The depth of meteoritic dust places earth age at ten or twenty thousand years.

• Oil deposits in the earth, evolutionists claim, were formed by heat and pressure acting on vegetation some eighty million years ago. Petroleum and natural gas are found in the earth under pressure, held in place by cap rock formations. These rock formations are permeable. Calculations indicate such pressure could not be maintained for more than ten thousand years.

• Atmospheric helium is produced in a measurable way. The amount of helium in the atmosphere, when all factors are considered, dates the earth from ten to twenty thousand years.

Again, most of the chemical processes indicate that the earth is thousands, not millions or billions of years, old. In fact, only a handful of theories indicate billions of years for the age of the earth. Of these, nearly all are the radioactive clocks.

Radiocarbon Dating

Carbon-14 dating techniques are falling into disrepute. The prestigious journal *Science* has reported stories of living snails mistakenly dated as 2,300 years old, wood taken from growing trees dated at 10,000 years old, and Hawaiian lava flows, known to be fewer than 200 years old, dated at three billion years (August 16, 1963; April 6, 1984).

One scientist, Robert E. Lee, writing in the *Anthropological Journal of Canada* (Vol. 19 [3]), expressed his scorn toward carbon-14 dating:

> Radiocarbon dating has somehow avoided collapse onto its own battered foundation. . . . The implications . . . are steadfastly ignored by those who base their argument upon the dates. . . . Why do geologists and archaeologists spend their scarce money on costly radiocarbon determinations? They do so because occasional dates appear to be useful. . . . Expressed in what look like precise calendar years, figures seem somehow better. . . . The radiocarbon method is still not capable of yielding accurate and reliable results. There are gross discrepancies, the chronology is uneven and relative, and the accepted dates are actually selected dates. "This whole blessed thing is nothing but 13th-century alchemy, and it all depends upon which funny paper you read."

Radiocarbon dating of fossils is based on the ability to measure the relative amount of carbon-14 contained in them. Carbon-14 is a radioactive isotope of carbon formed by the interaction of cosmic rays with atmospheric nitrogen. All living organisms contain carbon-14. Since it decays at a precise rate, we can supposedly determine the age of a fossil by comparing its present carbon-14 content with what it presumably had at death.

Several important assumptions must be made to use this method, however. Here are three:

1. We assume we know the amount of carbon-14 in the organism when it died.

2. We assume no natural process has altered the amount of carbon-14 in the fossil since the organism died.

3. We assume no phenomenon has affected the decay rate of carbon-14 since the death of the organism.

In discussing radiocarbon dating, the *Encyclopaedia Britannica* says carbon-14 is now known to be affected by such things as volcanic eruptions. In other cases, the mineral content of the water in the environment of marine animals can affect radiocarbon dates. It says the amount of carbon-14 in the atmosphere is affected by such things as industrial pollutants and nuclear bomb testing, which means that external conditions can alter the presence of carbon-14. While I find the *Brittanica* to be biased strongly in favor of evolution, it was interesting to read there: ". . . It is clear that carbon-14 dates lack the accuracy that traditional historians would like them to have." Other radioactive clocks, such as the potassium/argon clock, the uranium/lead clock, and the rubidium/strontium clock, also register similar problems and discrepancies.

Recent scientific discoveries are challenging the whole discussion of radioactive clocks. Evidence exists to challenge the thought that radioactivity is free from environmental influences. Recent experiments have demonstrated a change in the decay rate of radioactive materials. Laboratory changes in pressure, temperature, electric field, magnetic field and stress have been shown to affect the rate at which particles are ejected from the nuclei of atoms. Radioactivity may be affected by the presence of neutrinos in the atmosphere, which interact with the atoms' nuclei. Gange says:

> The phenomenon of radioactivity . . . could be [caused by] reactions occurring between neutrinos and particles within the nucleus itself. . . . This is important because eleven thousand years ago a pulsar . . . exploded and bathed the earth with an intense flux of neutrinos. If neutrinos affect the radioactive constant then the radioactive clocks we believe and trust today—which give billions of years for the age of things—may not be trustworthy at all. In which case the eighty natural processes which teach that the age of the earth is considerably younger than billions of years will emerge to remove the last vestige of evolutionary speculation.

Nine: Evolution As Growing Complexity

The mechanism of evolution depends on the concept that atomic particles sort themselves by chance into combinations of ever-increasing complexity. This concept means that order comes out of disorder through natural processes. This concept violates every observable natural phenomenon.

The second law of thermodynamics says every natural system, without the input of energy, moves from order to disorder. This is observed all around us. Metal mixes with oxygen in the air to produce rust. Rust never unmixes to produce shiny metal. Hot water and cold water mix to form lukewarm water. But lukewarm water never unmixes to produce hot water and ice-cold water. This is the process of *dis*integration: Things are falling apart and the universe is running down.

Ten: The Complexity of Human Cells

When evolution was proposed by Darwin, the biological understanding of the living cell was astoundingly simplistic. Since then, with the advent of electron microscopy, we have come to understand the human cell as a fantastic unit. With the discovery of the genetic code we have come to regard with awe the complexity of living systems. The information bound up within DNA specifies the human structure in minute detail. To register, much less to understand this complexity is beyond our ability.

As we look inside human cells, the organization takes on gargantuan proportions. Hemoglobin, for instance, is a protein found within the red blood cell. It is the agent that makes it possible to transport oxygen to all other cells in the body. Hemoglobin, just one of thousands of chemical substances in the body, is made up of four chains; each in turn is made up of a string of 140 amino acids arranged in a specific, invariable order.

The mathematical chance for the evolution of a system like hemoglobin (which is only a subsystem of a cell) is astronomical. It is more than astronomical; it is impossible, given the best scientific scenario, and the longest amount of time—five billion years. There simply is not enough time for the process to work itself out under the most generous scientific speculation.

This understanding has been underscored by a dispute between leading mathematicians and evolutionary biologists. Using computer models, mathematicians argue that laws of chance cannot explain the life we observe around us. Murray Eden, in a paper entitled "Inadequacies of Neo-Darwinian Evolution as a Scientific Theory," argues it would be unlikely "for even a single ordered pair of genes to be produced by mutations in . . . five billion years." Evolution could only occur, he said, if we could find a "new *determinative* feature" in science—in other words, a new natural law!

Conclusion

So bereft of evidence is the theory of evolution that many scientists are now taking another look at the possibility that God may indeed have created the universe. There is a new breed of scientists who believe the evidence suggests, based on their observation, that the universe was created as a place for man to be! This is called the Anthropic Principle, which states that the universe has been created with the intent of making it possible for mankind to exist. No less a light than English astronomer Sir Fred Hoyle, writing with Chandra Wickramasinghe, has suggested that life on earth was probably begun as a seed planted by higher intelligences from outside our galaxy or maybe even from God: "Once we see, however, that the probability of life originating at random is so utterly miniscule as to [be] absurd . . . it is therefore almost inevitable that our own intelligences must reflect . . . the higher intelligence . . . of God" (pp. 141, 144).

In the next two chapters we will consider the lie of occultism, which we will counter by exposing some of the hidden things of darkness.

10
The Idol of Occultism: Mystery Religion

The same forces that created modern secularism are also responsible for the widespread adoption of occultism in the Western world.

Both began when enlightenment thinkers overflowed the established channels of Catholicism in France, Lutheranism in Germany and the Church of England in Great Britain. Two streams of thought flowed out of the Enlightenment: The stream of secularism, as we have seen, left behind not only the Judeo/Christian spiritual foundations of Western civilization, but *all* spiritual influence as well; the stream of romanticism developed among those who were unable to see man merely as a machine and who sought to uncover a spiritual world outside the narrow confines of Western (biblical) theology.

The secularists could speculate that thought, love and art were the result of developments in the brain, but the romantics could not. They saw in nature something too wonderful to be explained by science. They were fascinated with the spiritual side of nature, but unwilling to be confined by theism. Their spiritual quest led them to the "hidden wisdom" of the ancients. They turned to Neoplatonism, which suggested mankind is basically an extension of nature. Human beings, the Neoplatonists said, exist in a body of flesh at the lower end of the cosmic spectrum. Their destiny is to rise through successively higher spiritual planes until they become pure spirit.

Neoplatonism is Western paganism. At its heart, it is no different from Eastern paganism—Hinduism. For our purposes all these terms are synonyms for the occult. Hinduism was born a thousand years before Plato speculated about the soul and its migration toward heaven from its fleshbound captivity. Let's look at Hinduism briefly to see the comparison.

Hindu philosophy begins with the idea of *Brahman*, the One Reality. The human soul is a projection of *Brahman*, and is, therefore, God. Classic Hinduism is essentially negative since it teaches that the soul is trapped in an endless cycle of birth, death and rebirth (*Samsara*). The law of *Karma* states that the condition of successive reincarnation is determined by the actions of previous lives.

About 500 B.C. Buddha, the Hindu prince, attained "enlightenment"—the final blessed state, free from both desire and suffering—while sitting under the fabled Bodhi tree. Buddha's enlightenment resulted from understanding Four Noble Truths: 1) Life is misery; 2) Misery comes from selfish desires; 3) Desire can be muted; 4) The process of muting misery consists of following a methodical path toward enlightenment. The methodical path became known as the Eightfold Path of Buddhism and included such endeavors as right speech, right thinking and right action.

Modern Hindu philosophy assimilates Buddhist salvation theology, suggesting that the cycle of birth and death may eventually be ended through some form of religious exercise such as meditation, good works or devotion to a particular god. Yoga, transcendental meditation and all other Eastern thinking, which penetrate the West through the teaching of various gurus, are all methods by which human beings can "become one with God."

At nearly the same historical moment Buddha was ascending in India, Plato was suggesting that the human soul could wend its way heavenward through philosophy. Perhaps Plato was influenced by Indian thinking. Certainly he came up with many of the same ideas the Indus River valley mystics taught. One similarity, as we noted earlier, was reincarnation or the transmigration of the soul. It wasn't until the third century A.D., however, that a man named Plotinus developed Plato's ideas into an organized system of philosophy that outlined the pathway by which the soul could ascend through various astral spheres to "the One" or "the Good." Later Neoplatonists decided they could not attain this oneness through philosophy alone. The *Encyclopaedia Britannica* describes it this way:

> Help from the gods was needed, and they believed that the gods in their love for men had provided it, giving to all things the power of return [to God] . . . implanting even in inanimate material things—herbs, stones and the like—. . . communications with the divine, which made possible the secret rites of [Greek magic].

Here we see the overtones of sorcery and alchemy, the manipulation of the "elements" (minerals, herbs and crystals, for example) in order to gain wisdom and power. When the romanticists turned to Neoplatonism, they were, in reality, turning to ordinary witchcraft. This was idolatry plain and simple, which they dressed up in philosophers' clothing and sold to the world, particularly the academic world.

Idolatry

These Enlightenment Neoplatonists could be called Neo-pagans; they merely penned a new chapter in idolatry. It was the same mistake made by "enlightened" thinkers in New Testament times. The apostle Paul, in the opening chapter of the book of Romans, described their error:

> Professing to be wise, they became fools, and changed the glory of the incorruptible God into an image made like corruptible man—and birds and four-footed animals and creeping things. . . . [They] exchanged the truth of God for the lie, and worshiped and served the creature rather than the Creator.   Romans 1:22–23, 25

Idolatry is the deification of that which is not God. It is the assignment of the power of God to abstract nature or to demons. The goal of idolatry is to induce mankind to submit to the lie of the devil in the Garden of Eden: that men may become gods. It is an attempt to dethrone God and enthrone man. Both Eastern and Western paganism boil down to sophisticated philosophical systems that enable mankind to evolve to godhood. When Neoplatonism, Hinduism, Mormonism, the New Age movement or witchcraft teaches methods for man to accomplish this evolution, it is advancing theories that are no different from the idolatry of the Philistines or Persians of Old Testament times.

The Roots of Modern Witchcraft

The romanticist occultists borrowed a wide variety of philosophies, all of which propelled them away from the revealed God of the Bible, instead exalting mankind. They experimented with spiritual power, a practice basic to rebellious human nature. Fascinated with the unseen world, they desired to manipulate it to their benefit. They did not understand that demon powers stand ready to offer forbidden wisdom to occultists and to reward their experimentation temporarily, but that they expect exorbitant payment. They require increasing submission and obedience from the occult practitioner. As Manly P. Hall has noted in his book *The Secret Teachings of All Ages:*

> Those who sought to control elemental spirits through ceremonial magic did so largely with the hope of securing from the invisible worlds either rare knowledge or supernatural power. . . . All forms of phenomenalistic magic are but blind alleys . . . and those who . . . wander therein almost invariably fall victims to their imprudence. Man, incapable of controlling his own appetites, is not equal to the task of governing the fiery and tempestuous elemental spirits. Many a magician has lost his life as the result.

Witchcraft and sorcery are the practical application of occult philosophy. Witchcraft, or ritual magic, is traced to ancient fertility rites when, for example, a barren woman would carve a figure of a pregnant woman to carry as an amulet or set up in her home. Magic was a common attempt to influence the gods to grant requests. Amulets and idols used in this way were a form of "sympathetic magic." Likewise, a tribe desiring a bumper wheat crop would erect a phallic symbol in the wheat field. They might then engage in sexual rites in the field, in the shadow of the phallus, to encourage the unseen powers to impart energy to the wheat. Occult religion established rules that attempted to influence the powers or gods. The sorcerer or witch or shaman was the guardian of the religious rituals. As societies became more formal, the witch doctors often became formalized into a priesthood. This happened very early in ancient Babylon, Egypt and India.

Judeo-Christianity was born in the midst of the worship of numerous local gods. God revealed Himself to Abraham and called him to monotheism. The first two of the Ten Commandments defined monotheism. So did the *Schema*, the declaration of Deuteronomy 6:4: "Hear, O Israel: The Lord our God, the Lord is one!"

God declares that He is not identical with nature; rather, He is the *Creator* of nature. He is the God who made man, loves him and communicates with him. God—ultimately revealed in Jesus Christ—is not to be approached through arcane study of the "weak and beggarly elements" (Galatians 4:9), but through the clear path of faith, described in the Bible: "When you did not know God, you served those which by nature are not gods. But now after you have known God . . . how is it that you turn again to the weak and beggarly elements . . . ? You observe days and months and seasons and years" (Galatians 4:8–10). The last sentence is a reference to astrology.

Witchcraft has changed little during the six thousand years of human history. The biblical admonition against it is clear:

> "There shall not be found among you anyone who
> makes his son or his daughter pass through the fire, or

one who practices witchcraft, or a soothsayer, or one who interprets omens, or a sorcerer, or one who conjures spells, or a medium, or a spiritist, or one who calls up the dead. For all who do these things are an abomination to the Lord."   Deuteronomy 18:10–12

The prophet Isaiah chastised the Israelites for their necromancy. God, he said, had forsaken them because of their fascination with Eastern mysticism:

You [God] have forsaken Your people, the house of Jacob, because they are filled with eastern ways; they are soothsayers like the Philistines. . . . Their land is also full of idols; they worship the work of their own hands.
                                                        Isaiah 2:6, 8

The temptation to idolatry did not end at the close of the Old Testament. Believers in the New Testament were in danger of being induced to forsake worship of God in Christ for "another" gospel. Paul expressed his fear that this would happen to the Corinthians:

But I fear, lest somehow, as the serpent deceived Eve by his craftiness, so your minds may be corrupted from the simplicity that is in Christ. For if he who comes preaches another Jesus whom we have not preached, or if you receive a different spirit which you have not received, or a different gospel which you have not accepted—you may well put up with it!
                                                   2 Corinthians 11:3–4

In the book of Colossians, Paul warned further against dabbling in occult practices and sophisticated worldly philosophies: "Beware lest anyone cheat you through philosophy and empty deceit, according to the tradition of men, according to the basic principles of the world, and not according to Christ" (Colossians 2:8).

The basic principles Paul referred to were the pagan philosophies of the Greeks and Persians of his day.

Neopagans Enter the Modern World

The romantic philosophers uncorked old wine—ancient "wisdom"—and its aroma spread throughout the modern world, intoxicating not only the religious, but most of the academic world. This basic shift was from theism to pantheism: God is not the Creator and sustainer of the universe, He *is* the universe. God ceases to be a personal Being but rather is identified as a spiritual *power* or *force* that is indistinguishable from creation.

The Enlightenment took the lid off a Pandora's box of occult deceptions. The new religious liberty of the romanticists, combined with a near-religious devotion to science by the secularists, allowed Western philosophers to stretch the envelope of spiritual thinking. Witchcraft—including sorcery and alchemy—was mixed with Hinduism and a form of unholy medieval Christian mysticism to form secret occult philosophical societies like Freemasonry and Rosicrucianism. Enlightenment romantics like Swedenborg and Goethe laid philosophical foundations for nineteenth-century occultists like Rudolph Steiner and Helena Blavatsky.

In the new pantheistic model, individuals were not rebellious and fallen. They were not sinful. Instead they were simply afloat in a physical, social and emotional process of evolution. The romantics saw the solution to human ills in education and social progress, not in redemption.

One of the most compelling assaults on the theistic traditions of Western society came as social scientists developed new definitions for the human soul. The animating force of human beings (which the Bible describes as the soul) began to be approached not by theology, but by the emerging science of psychology. Some romantics who explored the soul clearly crossed the line into witchcraft. Franz Mesmer, a Viennese physician who was influenced by the Renaissance mystic physician Paraclesus, attempted to develop a system of incorporating astrology into healing. He developed the theory of "animal magnetism," meaning that one person can transmit forces to others in sessions not unlike séances. Mesmer's animal magnetism would become modern hypnotism. Sigmund Freud's early work employed Mesmer's technique.

Psychology is a legitimate social science that explores human behavior—the way individual human beings react with their environment. The very root of the word *psychology* comes from the Greek word *psuche* or *soul*. The mistake some psychologists make is to assume it is possible to comprehend the inner workings of human beings from a non-theistic viewpoint. To explore the soul of man without God is to invite chaos. Human beings can be understood only superficially if we rule out the fact that they are created by a God who knows them, loves them and has plans for them.

Freud attempted to describe man's fear, guilt, hatred and love as a result of his repressed sexual feelings. Jung attempted to describe individuals as motivated by social and racial "archetypes." Both explanations are opposed to the Bible's position that man is a rebel and a sinner from birth, that he is terminally selfish, that he needs to face that condition realistically and turn to God and ask forgiveness.

The Bible, once the guide for human personal and social activity, was discarded by many seminaries and colleges by the early twentieth century. The new psychologists, who thought they understood humanity without a personal deity, began to treat the human soul from a pantheistic rather than a theistic viewpoint. Today modern science is split between the secular and the occult viewpoints. The humanities are overwhelmed by occultism. Current education models were heavily influenced by John Dewey (1859–1952) and reflect his conclusion that science has "cast into doubt the doctrines of sin, redemption, and immortality" (from Herbert Schlossberg's *Idols for Destruction*, p. 143).

As the twentieth century dawned, dusk settled over theism. William Manchester, describing the changes in England at the close of the Victorian era, said three forces replaced "religious evangelism": decadence, empty high Church or ritualistic Christianity, and rationalism (*The Last Lion*, Vol. 1., p. 197). Decadence and rationalism were two sides of the same coin of secularism; Christianity based on empty ritual reflected the penetration of paganism or mysticism into the Church.

The close of the nineteenth century saw the establishment of Freethinkers, Unitarians, Freemasons, Mormons, Christian Scientists and Madame Blavatsky's Theosophists.

Spiritualism was another broad, entrenched force flowing into the vacuum left by the removal of the Bible. Spiritualism grew out of the "folk magic" of New England when two young girls, the Fox sisters, began to receive messages from "departed spirits." During the last half of the nineteenth century, spiritualism numbered many distinguished men among its converts: John Ruskin, Sir Arthur Conan Doyle and English statesman William Gladstone. Spiritualism now describes an occult denomination that claims to be Christian, but it once was a synonym for what we call the occult. It included the followers of the Swedish Enlightenment mystic Emmanuel Swedenborg. Christian Science was another attempt to marry the occult and science with Christianity.

By the twentieth century, America was ripe for groups like Guy Ballard's I AM Movement. Ballard, filling lecture halls as he traveled through the United States in a caravan of cream-colored Cadillacs, claimed to share the secrets of the Great White Brotherhood, the so-called ascended masters of Theosophy, who supposedly initiated him on the heights of Mount Shasta. At Duke University J. B. Rhine, a psychologist, established a parapsychology department and coined the acronym ESP, for extrasensory perception, giving academic status to Neopaganism. By the 1950s countless denominations of "religious science" were selling various philosophies of mind over matter and positive thinking, like L. Ron Hubbard's Scientology. Wicca and other forms of witchcraft were coming out of the closet. The lines between Freudian/Jungian psychology, liberal Christianity, the human potential movement and the occult were nearly indistinguishable.

How Pervasive Is the Occult?

The final blow to Western theism came in the 1960s. By then the Bible had lost its authority for Americans. America publicly declared the biblical God dead. Not surprisingly, chaos mounted: The sparkling dreams of the 1950s were tarnished by rising crime, drug abuse, sexual immorality and, finally, Vietnam. Disillusioned baby boomers—robbed of the

Bible and searching for meaning—turned toward the East to welcome an array of saffron-robed gurus. Popular music declared, "This is the dawning of the age of Aquarius," and the Beatles brought us Maharishi Mahesh Yogi and through him transcendental meditation. Advocates of free sex, psychedelic drugs, homosexuality and "peace" discussed Zen Buddhism and meditation.

By the 1970s the joining of Eastern and Western paganism was complete. By the 1980s a new term was coined to describe the eclectic mix of psychology, liberal Christianity, Eastern mysticism and witchcraft—the New Age movement.

Marilyn Ferguson authored the seminal book for advocates of this new deception: *The Aquarian Conspiracy*. Describing the dawning of the New Age (supposedly marking the passage of the earth from the Piscean to the Aquarian astrological age) she wrote in 1980:

> A leaderless but powerful network is working to bring about radical change in the United States. Its members have broken with certain key elements of Western thought, and they may even have broken with history.
>
> . . . Broader than reform, deeper than revolution, this benign conspiracy for a new human agenda has triggered the most rapid cultural realignment in history. The great shuddering, irrevocable shift overtaking us is not a new political, religious, or philosophical system. It is a new mind—the ascendance of a startling world view that gathers into its framework breakthrough science and insights from earliest recorded thought.
>
> . . . There are legions of conspirators. They are in corporations, universities and hospitals, on the faculties of public schools, in factories and doctors' offices, in state

and federal agencies, on city councils and the White House staff, in state legislatures, in volunteer organizations, in virtually all arenas of policy-making in the country (pp. 23–24).

Today Eastern and Western paganism have flowed together to form a stagnant pool of deception that threatens to extinguish objective intellectual thought in the Western world. Pantheism reigns above the historic challenge to it. Witchcraft is practiced openly. Christian pastors commonly invite occultists to teach from their pulpits. Mediums (channelers) bring messages and "scripture" from demon powers. Rock music extols Satanism. Homosexuality is blatant. Abortionists cry out for the "freedom of choice" to murder the unborn. Drug abuse threatens the stability of the Western hemisphere. AIDS threatens to bankrupt our health care system. Violent crime makes the elderly prisoners in their homes. Large segments of our population are functionally illiterate. Welcome to the New Age.

Reaching the Occultists

To reach those lost in the occult, our greatest challenge is to unmask the devil. The occult is so insidious that Christians—even Christian leaders—are uninformed about it. The key to understanding the occult is to understand its general theological and philosophical underpinnings. To that end I dedicate the next chapter. Because the New Age is developing so rapidly and on so many fronts, it is impossible to be informed on every group and deception that springs up. It is not even possible to be well-informed on the largest groups.

In addition, the new occultism is anti-hierarchical. By that I mean we should not look for a structured association of New Age groups. In the first place, the devil is proud and occultists have little ability to submit to anyone, even each other. So those who look for a conspiracy among men are, I think, barking up the wrong tree. A conspiracy exists, but its management resides in hell.

Once we have become conversant with the general principles of occultism, we will rescue those trapped by it as we expose its fallacies. The key to winning occultists is to expose their systems, to show them for what they are—hollow, powerless shells in comparison to faith in Christ.

11
Confronting Occultism

We will reach occultists when we demonstrate that pagan religious practice will not overcome mankind's separation from God. Our approach to the occult must be rooted in our understanding that the Bible declares such practices to be abominable: "For all who do these things are an abomination to the Lord . . ." (Deuteronomy 18:12).

One need only look at ancient Egyptian occult religion and its fascination with the underworld—the realm of the dead—to see its darkness. Likewise, the gargoyles decorating Hindu temples (and even medieval cathedrals) speak to the darkness of the occult. The human sacrifices of Old Testament Canaanites, New World Aztecs and modern Satanists underscore the fact that evil never changes.

Because occult practice obscures the revelation of God, the key for dealing with the occultist is *to expose his dark practice:*

> Have no fellowship with the unfruitful works of darkness, but rather expose them. For it is shameful even to speak of those things which are done by them in secret.

> But all things that are exposed are made manifest by the
> light. Ephesians 5:11–13

The Greek word translated here as "exposed" is often translated "rebuke" or "reprove." There is a sense of prophetic
weightiness in the work of "exposing" dark things.

A similar thought was expressed in the Old Testament in
God's command to Ezekiel when He sent him up against the
rebellious house of Israel, which had fallen into idolatry. God
said He would put a word in Ezekiel's mouth that would
rebuke the children of Israel (Ezekiel 3:26–27). Similarly,
when Elijah faced the prophets of Baal on Mount Carmel, he
taunted them. When Baal would not light their ceremonial
fire, Elijah challenged them, "Cry louder [because he must
be] meditating, or he is busy, or he is on a journey, or perhaps
he is sleeping and must be awakened." God honored Elijah's
boldness and routed the forces of Baal.

Jesus Himself never shrank from exposing the dark work of
mankind. He said:

> "And this is the condemnation, that the light has come
> into the world, and men loved darkness rather than light,
> because their deeds were evil. For everyone practicing
> evil hates the light and does not come to the light, lest
> his deeds should be exposed. But he who does the truth
> comes to the light, that his deeds may be clearly seen.
> John 3:19–21

There often is an element of love-motivated confrontation
in exposing hidden things of shame. The apostle Paul reasoned with Greek philosophers in Athens and debated Scrip-

ture in the Jewish synagogue in Corinth, but when he came to Ephesus he entered into heavy spiritual warfare. There he went up against a firmly established occult community—worshipers of the goddess Diana. It was in this city that "God worked unusual miracles by the hands of Paul" (Acts 19:11) as he healed the sick and cast out evil spirits. The Bible account says:

> Fear fell on them all, and the name of the Lord Jesus was magnified. And many who had believed came confessing and telling their deeds. Also, many of those who had practiced magic brought their books together and burned them in the sight of all.   Acts 19:17–19

In bringing pagan philosophies to the light I am not suggesting that every encounter with paganism need be a Pentecostal showdown, although sometimes that is exactly what is required. The need for such bold confrontation came home to me when I was denied access to newspaper space to respond to a Mormon advertising supplement. I was told by the publishers of three newspapers that the Mormon message would be circulated, but my answer (which I had submitted to several pastors to be sure it was accurate and loving) would not be published. In effect I was told, "Freedom of the press belongs to him who owns one."

As I prayed about this situation, I had the strong impression that I was to picket the Idaho Falls Mormon temple. That was a radical thought, even for me. When I did that with about thirty of my church members, however, I not only got free television coverage on all three network affiliates, but one of the stations donated air time for me to debate a Mormon college professor of religion. As a result, I know of one woman who came to Christ and several other Latter-day Saints who were impressed enough by my television statements to say things to me like, "I can tell by listening to you that you are sincerely concerned about my soul."

Another example of this kind of bold encounter was related to me by Ed Decker, founder of Saints Alive! and author of the book (and movie) *The God Makers*. Ed was in the Philippines teaching a seminar on Freemasonry. As he lectured to a group of several hundred, a huge man walked up on the stage and stood with his arms crossed. When Ed was through, the man said, "I want you to come outside and talk to some guys." Ed confided to me later that he really didn't want to go!

Once he was outside a circle of Freemasons challenged him, asking him how he dared to come to their city and tell lies about Freemasonry.

"I'm telling no lies," Ed said. "And you know that. Now let me ask you a question. What is the Sacred Word of the Seventeenth Degree?"

"We won't tell you," they replied.

"Well," Ed said, "I'll tell *you*. It's *Abaddon*."

They were surprised he knew that. Seeing one of the men was carrying a Bible, Ed said, "Open your Bible to the book of Revelation and read chapter nine, verse eleven."

Here is what the man read: "And they had as king over them the angel of the bottomless pit, whose name in Hebrew is Abaddon, but in Greek he has the name Apollyon."

"Here you are claiming to be Christians and at the same time you go to the lodge, put on funny clothes and take upon yourself the name of the Destroyer! You need to repent."

The men knelt down on the blacktop and repented.

The Biblical Admonition

The book of Colossians was written to a people much like we are. They were Christians who were being tempted to give in to occult influences. Superspiritual people had apparently attempted to seduce them to return to idolatry. Paul wrote the letter to the Colossians to demonstrate the futility of worldly philosophy to add anything to the fullness of God as it is revealed in Christ:

> Beware lest anyone cheat you through philosophy and empty deceit, according to the tradition of men, according to the basic principles of the world, and not according to Christ. For in Him dwells all the fullness of the Godhead bodily; and you are complete in Him, who is the head of all principality and power.   Colossians 2:8–10

The pressure the Colossians faced was to take basic Christianity and add pagan philosophy to it. That early movement was known as Gnosticism, coming from the Greek word *gnosis*—"to know—to know hidden wisdom." Of the superspiritual mystics, who *thought* they had secret knowledge, Paul said:

> Let no one defraud you of your reward, taking delight in false humility and worship of angels, intruding into those things which he has not seen, vainly puffed up by his fleshly mind . . .   Colossians 2.18

Such occult wisdom—asceticism, vain ritual and empty mystical experience—Paul said, is of no use in real spiritual progress: "These things indeed have an appearance of wisdom in self-imposed religion, false humility, and neglect of the body, but are of no value against the indulgence of the flesh" (Colossians 2:23).

Paul understood that occultism was a ruse: It keeps people busy doing religious things in an attempt to improve themselves, but it doesn't deal with their real need—healing their spiritual separation from their Creator.

Strategy for Dealing with Occultists

Presenting the Gospel message in the face of complex religious practice can be a struggle. The Gospel message is always regarded by the superreligious as "too simple." The Bible warns us, however, that the devil works to seduce us away from "the simplicity that is in Christ" (2 Corinthians 11:3). Warfare against the occult is warfare between heaven and hell:

> The message of the cross is foolishness to those who are perishing, but to us who are being saved it is the power of God. For it is written: "I will destroy the wisdom of the wise, and bring to nothing the understanding of the prudent." . . . We preach Christ crucified, to the Jews a stumbling block and to the Greeks foolishness . . . (but) the foolishness of God is wiser than men.
>
> 1 Corinthians 1:18–19, 23, 25

The good news is that there is hope for reaching the occultist; *it is the very complexity of the occult message that makes the simplicity of the Gospel effective.* Exposing the hidden things of shame is often as simple as bringing the teachings of the occult out in the open. I was teaching a seminar in Livingston, Montana, recently. A man I'll call Roger came early to one of the meetings. He was from The Church Universal and Triumphant, an occult group that has purchased thousands of acres in Paradise Valley south of Livingston. The cult's leader, Elizabeth Clare Prophet, claims to be in touch with the Ascended Masters and to channel them. She has written the book *The Lost Years of Jesus*, which purports that Jesus went to live in India between the ages of twelve and thirty.

Roger, along with thousands of Elizabeth's devotees, "left the world" to come live in her shadow in Paradise Valley. He was a gentle little man who told me he was a Christian—that he "believed in Jesus." He couldn't understand why I would think he wasn't a genuine disciple of Christ. I questioned him about the so-called Ascended Masters who, according to Elizabeth Clare Prophet, were people like Jesus, Buddha, Mary Magdalene, Krishna and others. Roger said he believed they were all Ascended Masters and that he, too, could become one.

I asked him if I could read a portion of Scripture. He readily agreed. I read: "Jesus said to them . . . , 'I am the door of the sheep. All who ever came before Me are thieves and robbers' " (John 10:7–8).

I said, "Roger, the problem is, Jesus does not recognize any equals or any other 'Masters.' In fact, He condemns them all."

Roger looked at the verse, looked at me, smiled, then—lifting his finger to draw a mark in the air—said, "Well, that's one for you!" There was something innocent about him in that moment that made me feel caring toward him. I invited him to stay for the meetings. He came every night. When I last saw him he was leaving the church with a group of on-fire Christians, going out for coffee. The time we shared together at least got him to open his eyes to the possibility he had been deceived by the teachings of a false prophet.

Exposing hidden things of shame, in its simplest form, means bringing the practice out into the light and showing it for what it is. Following are several examples that demonstrate ways this can be done.

Transcendental Meditation

The Beatles not only introduced America to a new sound in the 1960s, they also brought us Maharishi Mahesh Yogi, an Indian guru promoting transcendental meditation.

TM is a Hindu method of "transcending" this illusory world. TM instructors consistently deny that transcendental meditation is a religious practice. They say it is simply a scientific technique in which one meditates on a one- or two-syllable Sanskrit word twenty minutes in the morning and twenty minutes in the evening. This practice is supposed to produce peace and creativity in the meditator. The May 3, 1990, issue of the *Seattle Post-Intelligencer* carried a half-page advertisement for TM. The ad said people wrongly associate TM with other Eastern practices. It says TM does not require "any change in your religion."

It's not that clear-cut, however. TM is *not* what its advocates say publicly it is. It is actually a specific form of Hinduism. When a person attends a lecture on TM, he will be told repeatedly that TM is not a religion, yet in order to receive his mantra (the Sanskrit word), he is required to go through a Hindu initiation ceremony. The initiate is asked to bring a clean white handkerchief, some fresh cut flowers and some fresh fruit to the ceremony.

For the ceremony he is led into a dimly lighted room where he stands, with his initiator, before a small table which is actually an altar, upon which is a picture of an Indian guru—

Shri Guru Dev. The initiator then begins to chant a long Sanskrit hymn. At various points during the chanting, he asks the disciple to participate—to spread out his white handkerchief, and later to place upon it his flowers and fruit. Here is the translation of part of the hymn (excerpts are taken from *Christianity Today*, March 26 and April 6, 1976):

> To the Lord Narayana, to lotus-born Brahma, the Creator . . . I bow down.
> . . . To the personified glory of the Lord, to Shankara, emancipator of the world, I bow down.
> To Shankaracharya the redeemer, hailed as Krishna and Badarayana . . . I bow down.
> To the glory of the Lord I bow down again and again, at whose door the whole galaxy of gods pray for perfection day and night.
> Adorned with immeasurable glory, preceptor of the whole world, having bowed down to Him we gain fulfillment. . . . [To] Brahmananda Sarasvati, the supreme teacher . . . Him I bring to my awareness. Offering the invocation to the lotus feet of Shri Guru Dev, I bow down. . . .
> Offering a cloth [handkerchief] to the lotus feet of Shri Guru Dev, I bow down. . . . Offering a flower to the lotus feet of Shri Guru Dev, I bow down. . . . Offering fruit to the lotus feet of Shri Guru Dev, I bow down. . . .
> . . . Guru in the glory of the great Lord Shiva, Guru in the glory of the personified transcendental fullness of Brahman, to Him, to Shri Guru Dev, adorned with glory, I bow down.

The initiate will then bow down before the altar, kneeling before the image of Guru Dev, and receive his mantra. He is told the mantra is one of hundreds, chosen for him to be psychologically and physiologically correct, but as you will see in a moment, this is not the case at all. For starters, all of the words given are *the names of specific Hindu gods!*

What is actually happening is that the TM initiate is unwittingly being indoctrinated into Hinduism. Maharishi himself said that through transcendental meditation one "rises to the level of divine Being, and it is [TM] that brings fulfillment to all religions" (*Transcendental Meditation*, p. 255). The purpose of meditation on the names of the gods is, according to Vedic (Hindu scripture) tradition, to call the spirit of that god into you to possess you so that it might aid you in transcending the world, to attain a state of creative intelligence, actually a state of nonbeing. Maharishi teaches that the TM practitioner "loses himself" until he is "One" with God: "He keeps on losing himself, but he does not know that he is losing himself and does not know even when he is completely lost. For, when he is lost, he is God; not even that he is God, but that God is God. Oneness of God consciousness, one eternal existence, oneness of eternal life, oneness of absolute Being; only the One remains (*Transcendental Meditation*, p. 283).

If we are to defeat the spread of religious ideas such as TM, we are going to have to bring these things out into the light. Most people, if made aware that they would be bowing down to Hindu gods, would never join TM. Americans who want to become Hindus are free to do so, obviously. But the Church must not sit by and allow people to be misled in religious issues without raising a voice.

Like all occult activity, the darkness of TM deepens with practice. Cult researchers Flo Conway and Jim Siegelman authored a book on occult/cult deception. In this book, *Snapping*, they report an interview with a former TM instructor. The man, called in the book Barry Robertson, said Maharishi purposely kept the "unenlightened masses" ignorant of TM's religious underpinnings. Robertson said:

> Deep down I knew I was lying to the public. I was lying when I said TM wasn't a religion. I was lying about the mantras—they weren't meaningless sounds, they were actually names of Hindu demigods—and [I was lying] about how many different [mantras] there were— we had sixteen to give to our students (p. 174).

TM does not stop with meditation. By 1980 you could take a course in levitation. More than five thousand people paid $5,000 to learn the TM "Sidhis" (perfection) technique. I remember viewing a TV newscast showing TM students sitting in the lotus position, bouncing up and down on thick foam rubber. They also bounced along a runway of foam rubber that suddenly stair-stepped up. They believed they would levitate eventually.

Questions We Should Ask

When encountering ideas that look a little "off," we should ask some questions. I'm convinced that most Christians are no longer thinking as critically as we should be. To illustrate this point, I often ask my audiences, "How many of you have seen a photograph of our galaxy, the Milky Way?" Invariably all hands go up. I then say, "There are no photographs of the Milky Way galaxy!" We think we know what our galaxy looks like. We believe that the Milky Way is a spiral galaxy, and so we draw pictures of it that way. But in order to take such a picture, we would have to leave our galaxy and photograph it from afar. My only point is, we can no longer afford to accept everything without first judging it.

Here are three questions I think can be helpful in confronting occult thinking:

1. *Does the end justify the means? Does it work?*

The occult is a quest for power. Witchcraft, for example, attempts to manipulate the universe to give someone what he wants. So-called "white magic" is an attempt to influence the powers, the "elements," the demi-spirits, to do one's bidding. Those who advocate a particular practice simply because "it works" are not going far enough in their thinking. Is the power legitimate power? Or has God declared it out of bounds?

2. *Is the practice natural or spiritual?*

Science is repeatable. When we give penicillin to cure infection, for example, we do so on the basis of objective testing. Any scientist who wants to perform the experiments can do so. But when it comes to the occult, we get into an area of faith. The practitioner must be an initiate. He must work his way up through lesser levels of expertise. This is clearly a spiritual dimension.

If it *is* spiritual, we remember that the spiritual realm is approached legitimately only through the name and blood of Jesus Christ, and under the warrant of Scripture. God has expressly forbidden every other doorway. The soul of man is the sole province of God.

When someone attempts to manipulate the mind, emotions and behavior of another without the ethical guidelines of Scripture and the approval of God, he embarks upon a dangerous road. Over and over again Scripture warns of the dangers of forbidden spiritual practices. Even objective secular researchers view the current prevalence of quasi-spiritual practice with skepticism. *U.S. News & World Report* writing on the New Age movement (February 9, 1987) observed: "From Manhattan to Malibu, a big and bizarre business is springing up as Americans look for supernatural answers to real-life problems. Psychics are collecting up to $250 an hour for making predictions and 'channeling' advice from entities, alleged spirits from another world or another time" (p. 67). Dr. Edwin Morse, former University of Wisconsin psychologist, warns that graduates of New Age thinking are often "psychically scarred."

3. *How good is the science?*

If the practice under consideration claims to be scientific, we should ask some questions. A man in Montana was promoting a new product recently to increase gas mileage. Actually he was selling an ordinary magnet to tape onto the gas line feeding the carburetor. The remarkable thing was that the magnets seemed to increase gas mileage! Stories of increased mileage circulated. The magnet was sold with a money-back guarantee if the purchaser did not notice at least a 10% increase in mileage. Eventually the drivers realized the reason their mileage went up was because as they followed instructions they were driving smarter: They were driving more slowly and they weren't jack-rabbiting away from stoplights.

The magnet merchant sold his wares through *stories* from people for whom the magnets had worked. This kind of scientific evidence is called "anecdotal." Anecdotes (stories) are not research. But unscrupulous people use anecdotal science to sell fatbuster pills, stop-smoking devices and self-improvement programs all the time. It's the snake oil salesman all over. As P. T. Barnum said, "There's one born every minute."

Often the anecdotes are accompanied by "conspiracy" theories. We are told that the new carburetor that will give us 200 miles per gallon is being held back by the oil companies who fear it will ruin their profits; the new cancer cure is opposed by the AMA because it is cheap and will put doctors out of business. The questions to ask when wondering about the quality of scientific evidence are "Specifically how does this work?" and "Let's see the objective reports from known and unbiased researchers."

Use these questions as a guide as you read through the next several examples. Ask yourself how you would go about documenting the claims of the disciplines. Then ask yourself if the practices might indeed touch on the occult.

Acupuncture

What is acupuncture? Most Americans have heard of it. Many have received acupunture treatment for a variety of ailments, or to help stop smoking or lose weight. The people I ask generally assume it has something to do with the nervous system: A needle is inserted into a nerve pathway, which interrupts pain or alters the flow of electro-chemical energy. That, however, is not what acupuncture is. Let's hear it from an acupuncturist, Dr. Ruth Lever, author of *Acupuncture for Everyone:*

> Acupuncture . . . is a single therapy, using the insertion of needles into the skin to treat a variety of ailments which might be treated by Western doctors with drugs or surgery. . . . The reason it is able to treat all ailments in the same way is because it sees them as stemming from the same cause—a disruption to the energy flow or vital force of the body (p. 11).

Well, our first question should be: "What is the vital force that acupuncture interrupts?" Dr. Lever confirms that it is the Oriental concept of *Chi* (pronounced chee):

The Chinese see the whole functioning of the body
and mind as being dependent on the normal flow of body
energy, or life force, which they call Chi (pp. 42–43).

Chi, Dr. Lever says, is a "universal energy which surrounds
and pervades everything." Furthermore, "My Chi is not dis-
tinct from your Chi." Chi is like light energy or radio waves,
but it cannot be seen or felt. And it does not disappear at
death: "There is a constant interchange between the Chi of
the body and the Chi of the environment" (p. 43).

Lever says the Chi force is related to the Eastern concept of
Yin and Yang. Chi circulates throughout the body along "meridians." These meridians cannot be located physically, nor
identified electronically. The description of the vital force of
the body sounds very much like the soul or the spirit. In fact,
the Oriental originators of acupuncture declared Chi to be the
spiritual essence of not only the body, but the universe.

It is obvious that the simplest exploration of acupuncture
demonstrates that it is a *spiritual,* not a *physical* phenomenon.
If it is a spiritual phenomenon, where is the Scripture sanc-
tioning it? Where is the protection of the blood of Christ in it?

Those involved in acupuncture are involved in spiritual
manipulation of the body. That is the essence of the occult.
There is not, in acupuncture, even the pretense of legitimate
science.

Many people ask about acu*pressure*. It is precisely the same
as acupuncture without the needles, using the same spiritual
"meridians."

Hypnotism

I was a student of hypnosis at an early age, and in high
school I would hypnotize my friends. Stage hypnotists per-

form remarkable demonstrations. And now extravagant claims are made for the benefits of hypnosis in health care and psychotherapy.

Hypnotism, as we have stated, is credited to the Enlightenment physician Franz Mesmer. Sigmund Freud became an early student of hypnosis when one of his patients slipped into a hypnotic trance of her own accord. (Freud eventually abandoned hypnosis in favor of psychoanalysis.)

Hypnosis is rooted in a theory that says the mind is divided into two realms: the conscious and the subconscious. Psychologists will often use the words *subconscious* and *unconscious* interchangeably, although *subconscious* may also refer to a different state of mental activity just below the threshold of consciousness. Freud postulated that psychological disorders could be accounted for by traumas that had occurred in a patient's childhood and had been repressed. By bringing these hidden memories to light, he hoped to effect cures in neurotic/psychotic behavior.

Today, popular opinion takes the subconscious for granted. Many therapies, including hypnosis, psychoanalysis and subliminal learning techniques, rest on the presupposition of the existence of the subconscious mind.

The theory of hypnosis states that the subconscious mind lacks the ability to make certain rational judgments. This is why, for example, the stage hypnotist can tell his subject that he is freezing and the subject will shiver, even though the room temperature is comfortable.

The theory of hypnosis states that we must get the message past the conscious mind to the subconscious. Thus the practice of hypnotism tries to distract the rational conscious mind to get the suggestion to the irrational subconscious.

It is the inability of the subconscious mind to make rational judgments that allows the hypnotherapist to make "posthypnotic suggestions." While under hypnosis, a smoker can be told he really doesn't like to smoke. Or an obese person can be told he will not experience hunger. Since the subconscious mind can't say, "Wait a minute. I *like* to smoke!" the subject—supposedly—can be freed from smoking.

Several problems exist in the theory of hypnotism:

The basic question is: "Is there such a thing as the subconscious mind?" This is a question most educated Americans probably would not think to ask, since the concept is so prevalent in our society. I think we need to ask it all the same.

The fact is, the theory of the unconscious mind is impossible to prove. *The Encyclopedia of Philosophy* (Vol. 8, p. 189) has a section devoted to this issue:

> We are dealing not with the mere existence of an entity which is untestable or conceptually impossible but with a theory . . . that does not stand for anything testable. . . . It would be pointless to prove the existence of the unconscious, even if such a proof were possible.

It is actually worse than that. We do not even agree upon what the mind is, let alone the subconscious mind. Quoting the *Encyclopedia of Philosophy:*

> The fact of the matter is that there does not as yet exist a very satisfactory account of our concept of the mind. We know that for each person a series of mental changes occurs, but if we try to say exactly what it is that changes we fall into utter obscurity. . . . Because of this inability to say what a mind is, many philosophers prefer not to speak of the mind as such (Vol. 5, p. 337).

So then the question one should ask at this juncture is "How good is the science?" Not only is the subconscious a philosophical impossibility to prove, but the concept of the mind itself is somewhat speculative. Have we ever seen a mind? Do we know where the mind is located? Is it in the brain? Is it in the heart? Is it—as some mystics believe—in the viscera? We are beyond science when we speculate upon how the subconscious mind works.

When considering this question we should inquire about the hard evidence for its effectiveness. Is it used widely in legitimate medical circles? The answer to that may be found in any good encyclopedia. The fact is, hypnotism, after two hundred years of experimentation, is regarded as low-result therapy at best. In "Limitations and Potentialities of Hypnosis," for example, written for the *Encyclopaedia Britannica* (under the general heading of *Hypnosis*), we read that hard evidence indicates that the objectively observed actions of the hypnotized are little different from those of the unhypnotized. Likewise, when unhypnotized subjects are asked to simulate hypnosis, their performance can deceive experienced hypnotists:

> A number of controlled studies . . . call many earlier
> extravagant claims about hypnosis into serious question.
> It now seems quite unlikely that the hypnotized person
> can transcend his waking potentials in physical strength,
> perceptiveness, learning ability, and productivity (Vol.
> 9, p. 138).

Another question: "Does the end justify the means?"
If, indeed, the subconscious mind is incapable of rational

thought, do we really want to feed it information without the protection of the conscious mind?

I can't help but think of the scriptural discussion about people who go too far in their speculation about these "elemental things." I think we are in danger of being cheated through philosophy by men "intruding into . . . things [they have] not seen" (Colossians 2:8, 18).

It is important to note that I am not suggesting that psychic or supernatural phenomena do not occur. On the contrary, I believe they do. My point here is that when such phenomena occur, they are better explained from a spiritual rather than a scientific viewpoint. If phenomena are spiritual, we must insist they be submitted to the authority of God's Word.

Subliminals

Another area of speculation currently in vogue is subliminal perception. The word *subliminal* refers simply to the claim that humans can perceive audio or visual messages that are below the conscious level of perception. That point in itself is not objectionable since people can perceive multiple stimuli at the same time. In other words, if I am watching TV and my wife speaks to me, I may hear her without really *hearing* her. The problem with subliminal teaching tapes is the conclusions they reach and the claims they make.

The whole discussion was projected into public view in a Fort Lee, New Jersey, movie theater in 1958. Jim Vicary, a researcher for the faltering Subliminal Projection Company, flashed high-speed Coca-Cola and popcorn messages on the movie screen so briefly that viewers couldn't consciously perceive them. He reported that Coke sales soared 18 percent and popcorn 57 percent. After repeated attempts to duplicate the results failed, he quietly recanted (*New York*, December 4, 1989).

The concept caught on, however, and, since then, a variety of products and services has been marketed to take advantage of subliminal perception. Double-Vision in Carson City, Nevada, makes plastic screens embedded with subliminal messages that can be plastered over televisions or windows (*New York*, December 4, 1989). Psychologist Lloyd H. Silverman of New York University insists that the words *Mommy and I are one*, when flashed subliminally, can tap into powerful unconscious wishes and provoke several types of improvement in behavior. Sometimes the messages are accompanied by a subliminal picture of a man and woman merged at the shoulders like Siamese twins (*Science News*, March 8, 1986).

The subliminal audiotape market has skyrocketed in recent years. Bookstore chains are devoting more and more space to them, offering help with losing weight, stopping smoking, getting rich and becoming sexually irresistible. One catalog advertises tapes with titles like *Flat Tummy Tape* ("I see my stomach lean, I see my stomach flat"); *Mother's Helper* ("I pick up after myself. I put things back where they belong"); *Flying without Fear* ("Flying is safe, I breathe deeply"); *I Like to List Real Estate* (presumably for a real estate agent who doesn't like to list real estate). According to *Psychology Today* (September 1988) one subliminal tape manufacturer, Potentials Unlimited, markets more than two hundred titles with sales of more than $6 million per year.

The messages may be recorded on several tracks at once, at several speeds and at several frequencies. The idea is that instead of getting a few hundred repetitions of the message per hour, one can "hear" the message tens of thousands of times.

As with hypnotism, the theory of subliminal perception relates to the power of the subconscious mind. Advocates of the technique have compared the conscious mind to that of a "rational guard," protecting the subconscious mind from messages it deems irrational. The technique of subliminal audiotape messages is to slip the message past.

Again, objective studies do not confirm the theories of subliminal perception. Frankly, the fact that the 1958 Coke and popcorn example is still the most quoted bit of scientific research on subliminals should raise questions in our minds. Howard Shervin, a University of Michigan psychologist who is a leader in subliminal research, says it's unclear what, if anything, people get out of subliminal tapes. He says they may even be harmful if people turn to them rather than more reliable sources of help. Of the tape companies who make exaggerated claims he says:

> It's a scam. Their catalogs refer to scientific research but omit specifics. When I write to ask for the evidence, they don't reply. If the results were there, wouldn't the tape companies be the first to cite them? (*Psychology Today*, September 1988).

Expelling Darkness

Occultists flourish. Benjamin Creme, one New Age guru, says the ultimate manifestation of the "Christ Spirit" is Lord Maitreya. Maitreya flew into London's Heathrow Airport with a Pakistani passport in 1977. Soon he was being proclaimed as a "master." Maitreya claimed one of his disciples was Jesus, who was living in a suburb of Rome. On April 25, 1982, Creme published full-page ads announcing that Lord Maitreya would soon appear on television simultaneously throughout the world declaring himself master and ushering in the New Age of peace. Maitreya, Creme said, is no different from us. He is simply further evolved. He is on his way to oneness with God in the Hindu tradition. Needless to say, Maitreya's magical television appearances never materialized.

The occult permeates our world. Channelers and gurus, mystics with magic methodologies, holistic healers and ascetics all hawk their brand of mystery Babylon religion. Our task is to be as informed as we can be, to be open to God's leading and to bear witness to a dark world of the light of Christ.

Sometimes the task seems impossible. We can, however, make a difference. One example can be seen in the recent change in the occult Mormon temple ceremony. For 140 years Mormons have been required to swear blood oaths not to reveal what went on in a Mormon temple. The Mormon put his thumb to his throat and drew it sideways from ear to ear swearing secrecy.

I have done this myself. I was a Mormon elder before I was born again in 1974. I went through the temple. Every time I did, I had to put my thumb to my throat in the occult blood oath, and swear not to reveal what went on in the temple. Practices like that are what make Mormonism as much a part of the occult as it is a cult.

A few years ago, however, a number of people began challenging Mormonism openly on this issue. Chuck Sackett published a book called *What's Going On in There?*, exposing the temple ceremony. Ed Decker produced a movie called *The Temple of the God Makers*. (We used to show it on Main Street in Salt Lake City in the summer as part of our street evangelism program at the Capstone Conference.) Finally, Bill Schnoebelen and I published *Mormonism's Temple of Doom*, which contained a detailed description and an explanation of the occult nature of the temple ceremony. We also announced the publication of our book *Whited Sepulchers*, which locates and describes the occult symbols that festoon the Salt Lake City Temple.

In the spring of 1990 the Mormon Church dropped the blood oaths. They made no explanation for their decision. I am convinced that when we uncovered the occult roots of the ceremony and exposed it to the world, the light dispelled the darkness.

Our job in encountering the occult is to take the light of the Gospel of Christ to this present dark world. When we do that, some will be liberated from false systems of darkness.

12
The Idol of Cultism: Another Jesus

Our third grouping of hard cases involves cults. A cult is a religion viewed as unorthodox by the parent group from which it splintered. In the Western world, the cults we are interested in broke from the religions based on biblical revelation. Cults have spunoff from Judeo-Christianity from the beginning: The Old Testament is a history of Israel's turning to follow pagan gods under the leading of false prophets. Moses had to contend with the "strange fire" of Nadab and Abihu (Leviticus 10:1, KJV). When Jeremiah lamented over the teaching of false prophets, God said:

> "The prophets prophesy lies in My name. I have not sent them, commanded them, nor spoken to them; they prophesy to you a false vision, divination, a worthless thing, and the deceit of their heart."   Jeremiah 14:14

One of the primary messages of the New Testament epistles is warning against heresy; nevertheless, down through the centuries come the bearers of strange fire. Though their messages vary widely, they contain many similarities. Those become apparent in an overview of cult groups.

● On April 14, in 216 A.D., a twelve-year-old Persian boy living in southern Babylonia claimed that an angel appeared to him in the yard behind his home. The boy, Mani, had been raised in a legalistic Christian sect known in those days as the "Baptists." Mani said the angel told him God would restore the One True Church through him. Manicheanism lasted five hundred years and spread throughout the Roman Empire, teaching a legalistic system of personal righteousness, adding new "scripture," sending missionaries out two by two to teach secret temple ceremonies. Augustine (who became St. Augustine) was a member of the Manicheans for ten years until he was converted.

● In 610 A.D., in a cave outside Mecca, Muhammed also received a visitation from an angel, later identified as Gabriel. Gabriel supposedly said God would restore true religion through Muhammed. Muhammed had been raised in a pagan society, but in travels to Syria he was deeply affected by the Jews and Christians he encountered. Thus, Islam grew out of the Bible stories Muhammed heard about Abraham. Muhammed decided Abraham's son Ishmael (whom Bible students agree is the father of Arabs) was Abraham's legitimate heir rather than Isaac.

● During the Middle Ages, the heavy authoritarianism of the Roman Catholic Church firmly resisted attempts to establish breakaway Christian groups, often killing the leaders in an attempt to resist heresy. After the Protestant Reformation, when religious liberty began to be established as a principle of government in the Western world, a multitude of new Christian groups formed. In America, quasi-Christian cults began in the wake of the Second Great Awakening (1787–1825) following the Revolutionary War.

• In 1820 Joseph Smith, the founder of Mormonism, recounted an angelic appearance reminiscent of both Mani and Muhammed. His story (which evolved greatly during the following 25 years) arose out of his family's disenchantment with existing Christianity and his fascination with the occult. (See my book *Have You Witnessed to a Mormon Lately?*, chapter 3.)

• Mary Baker Eddy, the founder of Christian Science, was born in 1821 and raised in a stern Calvinistic home. From an early age she was troubled with the idea that God would eternally punish sinners. When in middle age she came into contact with Phineus T. Quimby's teaching, "The Science of the Christ," she began a study that ultimately produced her new denomination.

• Charles and Myrtle Fillmore were also influenced by Quimby, founding the Unity School of Christianity in 1895. The Fillmores, Eddy and Quimby himself all drew upon what has come to be called "New Thought" to round out their theologies.

New Thought was a popularism of an earlier movement throughout New England, sometimes called New England Transcendentalism. The New England Transcendentalists, including Ralph Waldo Emerson and Henry David Thoreau, gave voice to the liberalism that began in the Enlightenment. In New England a terrible war was waged between biblical Christianity and the new Christian/social/psychological liberalism infiltrating the American Church as deism died out. In

1819 William Ellery Channing began another offshoot movement known as Unitarianism.

New England in the nineteenth century was a hotbed of religious experimentation. Orthodox churchmen spoke of New England as "the psychic highway." Presbyterian evangelist Charles Finney referred to the area as the "burnt-over district." Such movements as Mormonism, Shakerism, spiritualism and the sexual communism of the Oneida Community were birthed there.

• Like Mary Baker Eddy, Charles Taze Russell (1852–1916) was raised in a Christian home but disliked the idea of eternal punishment. In 1870 Russell attended an Adventists meeting in Allegheny, Pennsylvania, and was fascinated with the idea of Christ's imminent return. As Russell pursued his preaching and teaching, his doctrinal positions became increasingly distinctive, until he declared it was impossible to understand the Bible without his organization's—Jehovah's Witnesses'—*Watchtower* publications.

Cults continue to proliferate. Sun Myung Moon founded the Unification Church and Victor Paul Wierwille started The Way International in response to visions. Herbert W. Armstrong was convinced he had the whole truth for the whole Church when he founded The Worldwide Church of God. Some of these sects fell apart quickly: David Berg's Children of God, once thought to be the beginning of a major cult, is headed for a fizzle. Many other smaller groups flourish for a season before they sink into history.

When Is a Cultist Not a Cultist?

Cults are difficult to deal with, precisely because they have their roots in the Church. The cult terminology is often tricky. They use the Church's words for their theological ideas but assign their own meanings to them.

It is always a mistake to assume we know precisely what a person believes because he is a member of a particular group. While we can suspect he believes certain things, we need to listen carefully. We are concerned with truth and doctrinal purity, not with labels.

Sometimes Occultists Masquerade as Cultists

Sometimes the dividing line between cults and the occult is thin. Mormonism is a good example. Mormonism is normally thought of as a quasi-Christian cult. Indeed, Mormons use the King James Version of the Bible, refer to the atonement of Christ, baptize, take a form of Communion, and even say they believe in the Trinity (closer examination demonstrates they do not).

But at the heart of Mormonism is the belief that people may eventually become gods by observing Mormon law. This belief stems from Joseph Smith's overt occult activity. Smith was deeply rooted in the occult. Likewise, Mary Baker Eddy, though she used Christian terms, basically started an occult group, not a cult group. The occult influence of the New England Transcendentalists is felt in these groups.

Many Latter-day Saints are deeply involved in the occult. Numerous Mormon chiropractors and naturopaths are rooted in unscientific "holistic" healing practices. The occult Mormon Temple ceremonies create an openness to the spirit world in ways condemned by the Bible. One Mormon prophet, for example, said all the founding fathers of the United States "visited" him in the St. George Temple in Utah. When I am talking with a Mormon who is focused upon becoming a god, I treat him as an occultist. (I furnished examples of that in the section on the occult.)

Sometimes Secularists Masquerade as Cultists

Many Mormons, on the other hand, are secularists. They become Mormons because Mormonism teaches decent human values and strives to maintain family unity. I call these people liberal Mormons. They remind me of former Mormon church historian Leonard J. Arrington who, writing in a liberal Mormon journal, said he was not "overly concerned" with the reality of Joseph Smith's visions. He said he was prepared to accept Mormon, Christian and Hebrew Scripture stories as "historical, metaphorical, or symbolical." To demonstrate his broadmindedness Arrington quoted an Italian proverb: "Whether it is literally true or not, it's still true."

So, we cannot approach all cultists in precisely the same way.

The Problem of "Cultishness"

You can't judge a book by its cover. It's easy to assume people have come to saving knowledge of Christ because they claim to be Presbyterian, Baptist, Pentecostal or Methodist.

The very concept of wolves in sheeps' clothing (Matthew 7:15) speaks to the idea of "cultishness." Cultishness is the no man's land between orthodox Christianity and clearly identifiable cults. Here Christian individuals, congregations or denominations subscribe to doctrinal positions that either are harmful or lead to harmful consequences.

I believe this witnessing area is the most difficult for Christians. I know it is for me. I certainly do not want to be narrow or bigoted. I do not want to stain a brother's reputation. I do not want to call unclean that which God has called clean (Acts 10:15). I move with fear and trembling in this area.

A friend used to say the first marks of the cults would be found in "a day, a diet or a doctrine." He meant we could look for cultishness in teachings that focused on peripheral issues until the central message about Christ was damaged. Taking a portion of Scripture and emphasizing it to distortion is sometimes called "majoring on minors." I believe this is the essence of Paul's warning to us:

> So let no one judge you in food or in drink, or regarding a festival or a new moon or sabbaths, which are a shadow of things to come, but the substance is of Christ. . . . Why . . . do you subject yourselves to regulations—"Do not touch, do not taste, do not handle". . . ? These things indeed have an appearance of wisdom . . . but are of no value against the indulgence of the flesh.   Colossians 2:16–17, 20–21, 23

Bad doctrine produces tainted fruit. A common manifestation of this is seen in people who have genuine experiences with Christ, yet receive unorthodox teaching. While it may not separate them from Christ, it shows up in the second generation. Everyone is familiar with stories of legalistic or "hard" Christians who manage to destroy their children's chances for conversion.

Does our responsibility as evangelists stop as soon as we are convinced someone is saved? I think not. In the Great Commission we are told to make disciples of all the nations. Our work is not done when someone says the sinner's prayer. Paul said he was "innocent of the blood of all men" because he had "not shunned to declare . . . the whole counsel of God" (Acts 20:26–27).

I am asked often about groups that seem to be on the fringes of the Church. The real nature of heresy is that it divides the Church. When a group majors on a minor point so that it becomes a test of faith, it is in danger of heresy.

An example of this kind of splitting has been seen among the Seventh-Day Adventists. For years this denomination separated itself from the rest of the Body of Christ. Likewise, the Church distanced itself from Adventists because of their legalistic insistence upon Saturday worship (sometimes even identifying Sunday worship as "the mark of the beast"), their dietary restrictions and the elevation of their prophetess Ellen G. White. Today Seventh-Day Adventists are trying to minimize the differences between themselves and evangelical churches. Many doctrinal problems, however, continue to impede full fellowship. Their legalistic approach to salvation, for instance, is problematic.

Other groups, like some of the non-instrumental Churches of Christ, take a highly legalistic view of water baptism. Some independent Pentecostal churches elevate the gift of tongues as a sign of *salvation*. Such groups skate dangerously closely to the edge of cultism.

Another group that seems to exist in the gray edges of the larger Church is the United Pentecostal Church. I have spent hours in discussion with UPC pastors. For the most part I find them delightful brothers. They are, however, split over the biblical understanding of the nature of God. Half believe in the biblical "three-in-one" God but balk at the word *Trinity*. While they believe—once the terminology is sorted out—what the rest of the Church believes, they choose to call that belief "Oneness." Another half of them are clearly non-Trinitarian in doctrine as well as name. They are unitarian. I will speak to these distinctions in the next chapter.

Then there are groups that call themselves "Baptist," "Pentecostal" or "Church of Christ," but are unorthodox. Many, perhaps most, of these people are orthodox brothers and sisters in the Lord. Some, however, have allowed their particular doctrines to separate them from the Body of Christ. I remember having a dialogue with one such Church of Christ minister. I told him that I had exercised faith in Christ, repented of sin and been water-baptized by immersion. I testified to a changed life and a daily walk in fellowship with Jesus. In his eyes, however, none of that made me a Christian. He said I needed to be re-baptized and to stipulate that I was being baptized in order to *become* a Christian, not because I *was* a Christian.

I must include in the gray area those who have allowed their liturgy to replace relationship. Many Protestants and Catholics have reduced Christianity to a dead formula. Then there are those we sometimes call Christian liberals. By them I mean those for whom God is far away: The blood of Jesus has lost its power, the Word of God its authority.

Cultishness is the bane of the Church. Organizations, intermediaries and formulas replace vibrant relationship with the Lord Himself. Jesus speaks of impotent churches in the book of Revelation: "You have left your first love" (2:4); "committed sexual immorality" (2:14, 20); "have a name that you are alive, but you are dead" (3:1); "are lukewarm" (3:16).

I realize that even bringing up the concept of cultishness will make some people uncomfortable. But I am motivated by the fact that doctrinal walls sag before they collapse. Unhealthy trees produce little fruit and often the fruit is unwholesome. We who truly worship the Father are required to do so both in spirit and *truth* (John 4:23). "The truth," Jesus said, "shall make you free" (John 8:32).

A Warning About Deception

When I do seminars I usually open the last session for questions and answers. In a small Oregon town one meeting was dominated by questions from a very nice man who was perplexed by the fact that Christians considered his church a cult. As he described his beliefs, it became apparent to the vast majority of those present that his beliefs were indeed unorthodox. Reason as we could with him, we could not break through to common ground. Yet he was so sincere!

One woman thought I had been too insistent with the man. But was I? While we cannot look into another person's heart, we should not think that everyone who appears sincere is not deceived. Aren't mentally disturbed people sincere when they report conversations they think they have had with Napoleon or George Washington? We need to remember Jesus' admonition to be "wise as serpents" while we are being "harmless as doves" (Matthew 10:16). What this woman did not realize was that I had already spent five hours with the man prior to the meeting. He was, in my judgment, not looking for truth at all. I believe he was completely deceived and, in some ways, dangerous to the Body of Christ. Certainly he was dangerous to those who were not grounded in their faith.

The moral of this story is that we must stay alert spiritually, not only for our own sakes, but for those who are counting on us to protect them from error. This point is underscored for me by the number of letters I receive from pastors who have lost their own children to the cults. Their failure was in being gentle but not wise.

When we encounter the cults we are dealing with dark spiritual powers. The Bible is replete with warnings about the coming of false prophets. Paul said false prophets go into great detail over things they have not really seen. They become puffed up and lose contact with God (Colossians 2:18). These kinds of false apostles are

> deceitful workers, transforming themselves into apostles of Christ. And no wonder! For Satan himself transforms himself into an angel of light. Therefore it is no great thing if his ministers also transform themselves into ministers of righteousness.   2 Corinthians 11:13–14

Because of the danger of false angelic messengers, Paul warned us:

> If we, or an angel from heaven, preach any other gospel to you than what we have preached to you, let him be accursed. As we have said before, so now I say again, if anyone preaches any other gospel to you than what you have received, let him be accursed.   Galatians 1:8–9

One Sure Mark of the Cults

The frantic message of lying spirits is that *Jesus is not God.* He can be a great teacher, a prophet, an ascended master, the "son" of God or even "another god." The devil knows that when individuals see the triune God clearly, they will be changed in a fundamental way (2 Corinthians 3:16–18). The devil loses his power over those who see Jesus and receive Him.

Jesus unfolded the revelation of His nature to the Jewish leaders carefully. When they finally understood the implications of His message, they killed Him because He made Himself "equal with God" (John 5:18).

Jesus told them: "You search the Scriptures, for in them you think you have eternal life; and these are they which testify of Me" (John 5:39).

The religious leaders of Jesus' day could tolerate anything He said or did except His insistence that He was God. They took up stones to stone Him when He used the *I AM* designation for Himself. The *I AM* title was the name of God revealed to Moses in the desert. When Jesus told the Jews, " 'Most assuredly, I say to you, before Abraham was, I AM.' Then they took up stones to throw at Him" (John 8:58–59).

The Bible's most fundamental purpose is to reveal God. The Old Testament prepared us for Christ. The New Testament records His appearance. The implications of that appearance are without comparison. As we read the Gospel of John, we see Jesus purposefully revealing Himself in progressively clearer declarations. When in John 10:30 He said, "I and My Father are one," the Jews "took up stones again to stone Him." When He asked why they were set on killing Him, they replied that it was because "You, being a Man, make Yourself God."

When Jesus was arrested in the Garden of Gethsemane, He asked the officers sent from the chief priests and Pharisees, "Whom are you seeking?" They replied, "Jesus of Nazareth." He said, "I am He." At that response, the troops were thrown to the ground (John 18:4–6).

Finally, Jesus was brought before the Jewish ruling Sanhedrin, led by Caiaphas, the high priest. A false witness testified that Jesus claimed He could rebuild the Temple of Solomon in three days. Caiaphas asked Jesus if He was the Christ. Jesus said, "I am" (Mark 14:62).

Caiaphas was outraged by this response: "The high priest tore his clothes, saying, 'He has spoken blasphemy! What further need do we have of witnesses? Look, now you have heard His blasphemy!' " (Matthew 26:65).

The cults, likewise, offer a Jesus who is not God. Mormonism teaches that Jesus is "another" god; Jehovah's Witnesses teach that Jesus is the "first creation of God"; Sun Myung Moon teaches that Jesus is one manifestation of Christ (who failed fully to save mankind); and Victor Paul Wierwille wrote—as a foundation for The Way International—the book *Jesus Christ Is Not God.*

The cults want to retain the title *Christian.* In every case they claim to be the real Christians. Everyone else has departed from the truth. They alone are the way back to God. Since they attack the deity of Christ, it is our responsibility to defend His deity. The purpose of the next chapter is to provide you with the biblical information to do that.

13
Confronting Cultism

The Pharisees resented Jesus Christ. They objected to His healing on the Sabbath (Matthew 12:9–14), His fellowship with sinners (Matthew 9:11), His disdain for their religious traditions (Mark 7:5). Most of all they resented His claims of divinity and, as we saw in the last chapter, crucified Him for those claims. In their determination to ruin His reputation and tempt Him into blasphemous statements, they sent scribes to trap Him with carefully crafted questions. On one such occasion He turned the tables on them:

> While the Pharisees were gathered together, Jesus asked them, saying, "What do you think about the Christ? Whose Son is He?" They said to Him, "The Son of David." He said to them, "How then does David in the Spirit call Him 'Lord,' saying: 'The Lord said to my Lord. . . .' If David then calls Him 'Lord,' how is He his Son?" And no one was able to answer Him a word, nor from that day on did anyone dare question Him anymore.   Matthew 22:41–46

With this query, Jesus pointed to an essential question about His nature. He did *not* ask the Pharisees if they thought He was the expected Messiah. He asked instead about the *nature* of the Messiah: Would the Messiah simply be a human descendant of David, merely a man with a spiritual anointing? Notice this distinction: The Jews did not give Jesus over to death for claiming to be the Messiah, but for claiming to "be equal with God" (John 5:18; 10:30–33).

The Divinity of Christ

The hallmark of the cults is their attempt to destroy the full deity of Jesus; the hallmark of orthodox Christianity is its declaration that Jesus is fully God, as well as fully man. For twenty centuries the Church has made a reply to the question "Who is Jesus Christ?" Our answer: Jesus is God incarnate— God come in the flesh.

The idea of Jesus the God/man has been hotly contested. Much of the content of the great creeds of the Church came about in the face of challenges to this concept. The Council at Nicea in 325 A.D. defended Jesus' full deity in the face of the Arians who claimed Jesus was not God but was the first being God created (as Jehovah's Witnesses believe today). And important doctrinal battles were fought about His humanity. Some groups viewed Jesus as a manifestation of God who only "appeared" to be human. Still other problems arose over how Jesus' appearance as God in the flesh affected our overall notions about God: Did the Father stop being the Father to become the Son?

It is not my intent to try to identify all of the various ways scholars have thought about the relationship between the Father and the Son. For our purposes I want to demonstrate that the primary mistake of the cults is to miss Christ's full deity. If we are aware of *that* error and are prepared to address it, we will be able to speak with authority to the central problem in the major cult groups.

There is a secondary error (discussed in the last chapter) called the "Jesus-only" movement. Where tritheism makes Father, Son and Holy Ghost into three gods and destroys the essential unity of God, unitarianism (referring not to the organization but to the Jesus-only doctrine) allows Jesus to be God, but at the expense of the Father and the Holy Spirit. In order to discuss these issues at all, we must establish the biblical definition of God. We will then show how the Bible teaches that Jesus possesses all the attributes of God.

The Nature of God

Why is the accurate understanding of the nature of God so important?

Doctrinal error destroys the unity of the Church. Christian brotherhood, our common life in fellowship in Christ, is central to establishing the Kingdom of God on the earth. Jesus' purpose was to redeem mankind from the curse of sin and establish the Kingdom of God "on earth as it is in heaven." In establishing His Church, He prayed we would "all be one" (John 17:21). He also said our love for each other would demonstrate to all that we are His disciples (John 13:35), an obvious aid in establishing His Lordship. Paul recognized the importance of doctrinal unity. He said gifted teachers of the Gospel would bring us into the

> unity of the faith and of the knowledge of the Son of God
> . . . that we should no longer be children, tossed to and
> fro and carried about with every wind of doctrine

> . . . but, speaking the truth in love, may grow up . . .
> into Him who is the head—Christ.   Ephesians 4:11–15

Our salvation (which includes our eventual full spiritual, emotional and physical healing) comes from knowing God as He really is. Peter said what we need for life and godliness is wrapped up in our knowledge of God (2 Peter 1:3). Something happens to us when we see God accurately, when we come to *know* Him. Paul went so far as to say that when we worship God rightly, something important happens to our own nature: We are "transformed" (2 Corinthians 3:18). Error clouds our vision of Him and obscures our understanding of Him. When the cults *obscure* God's nature they frustrate mankind's redemption. For these reasons, cultish error is not some musty intellectual or doctrinal issue.

We need to be skeptical of superficial definitions of God's nature. When a cultist tells us he believes in God, or that he is a Christian, we need to ask what he means by that statement. When Paul said, "No one can say Jesus is Lord except by the Holy Spirit," he did not mean that no nonbeliever can mouth those words. Nor did he mean that anyone who says those words is born again. The confession "Jesus is Lord" is really the earliest creed of the Church. In order for the phrase to have any meaning at all, we must define both terms: *Jesus* and *Lord*. But even before that, we must look at our understanding of God Himself.

The Definition of God

To defend the proposition that Jesus is God, we will first define what we mean by God. That may seem elementary, but it is essential. When a Mormon says Jesus is God, for example, he really means Jesus is one of a multitude of gods. In Mormonism people may become gods.

Historically, orthodoxy has taught certain minimums about God. We have identified His attributes. Among other things, God is holy, just, loving and merciful. We also speak of God's nature. In so doing, it is common to think of God in three primary ways. He is omnipresent (everywhere present), omnipotent (all-powerful) and omniscient (all-knowing).

God Is Omnipresent

God is the God of heaven and earth (Genesis 14:19), not only because He created them (Genesis 1:1), but because He actively reigns over them. Christianity teaches a God who not only created the universe, but who is intimately involved with every aspect of it. He is available and accessible immediately through prayer, because He is omnipresent. "Am I a God near at hand," says the Lord, "and not a God afar off? Can anyone hide himself in secret places, so I shall not see him?" says the Lord; "Do I not fill heaven and earth?" (Jeremiah 23:23–24).

Moses recognized that God is "in heaven above and on the earth beneath" (Deuteronomy 4:39). Likewise, David extolled God's omnipresence: "Where can I go from Your Spirit? Or where can I flee from Your presence? If I ascend into heaven, You are there; If I make my bed in hell, behold, You are there" (Psalm 139:7–8).

God "sits above the circle of the earth . . . stretches out the heavens like a curtain, and spreads them out like a tent to dwell in" (Isaiah 40:22). "Heaven is My throne," He says, "and earth is My footstool" (Isaiah 66:1).

God Is Omnipotent

His power is total. When God promised Abraham that his ninety-year-old wife, Sarah, would conceive a son, she laughed. But God asked patiently, "Is anything too hard for the Lord?" (Genesis 18:10–14). God sent the angel Gabriel to tell Mary she was to conceive Jesus miraculously by the power of the Holy Spirit. As Gabriel explained this to Mary—and told her further that her elderly relatives would soon have a son as well—Gabriel said, "With God nothing will be impossible" (Luke 1:37).

God is Creator of the physical universe. He made the heavens and the earth (Genesis 1:1); He founded the world according to His wisdom and stretched out the heavens by His understanding (Jeremiah 51:15); He possesses absolute dominion and authority in heaven and earth (Isaiah 37:16); "all things" were made by God (John 1:3).

The Old Testament prophet Amos says God made the constellations Pleiades and Orion (Amos 5:8). God created simply by willing to do so (Revelation 4:11). The writer of Hebrews tells us God made the worlds by His word: "We understand that the worlds were framed by the word of God, so that the things which are seen were not made of things which are visible" (Hebrews 11:3).

God's power, in addition, extends over life itself. He is Lord of and giver of life. He gives breath and spirit (Isaiah 42:5). As "the Father of us all" He exercises sovereign rule over all life. He is the God "who gives life to the dead and calls those things which do not exist as though they did" (Romans 4:17).

God Is Omniscient

God calls Himself the Alpha and the Omega, the beginning and the end. As the all-knowing Creator, God is the originator of all wisdom.

God "searches all hearts and understands all the intent of the thoughts" (1 Chronicles 28:9). "For the eyes of the Lord run to and fro throughout the whole earth, to show Himself strong on behalf of those whose heart is loyal to Him" (2 Chronicles 16:9).

The Progressive Revelation of God

The Bible reveals the nature of God through a series of progressive revelations. After mankind's failures in the Garden of Eden and on the plains of Babylon, God again revealed Himself to Abraham. Through Abraham, God began to separate out a people who would worship Him rightly. The Old Testament is the story of God calling His people, the Jews, away from idolatry. The Gentile nations who opposed Israel were pagan polytheists. They worshiped numerous demon gods. In the face of polytheism, the Old Testament message was, There is only one God.

In the Old Testament, through His dealing with the Jewish people, God continued to reveal grand aspects about His nature: His love, His mercy, His justice, His patience and even His wrath. Often He would reveal a new aspect of His nature and, at the same time, coin a new word to describe Himself: *Jehovah-Jireh* (Our Provider); *Jehovah-Shalom* (Our Peace); *Jehovah-Tsidkenu* (Our Victory Banner); and *Jehovah-Rapha* (Our Healer).

The Jews did not understand the revelation of God in the Person of Christ. The Jewish rulers of Jesus' day did not possess a genuine relationship with God, because if they had, they would have recognized His appearance in the flesh. Jesus told them, "If God were your Father, you would love Me" (John 8:42).

The Christological Problem

As we read the Old Testament we become firmly convinced that there is only one God. Any other concept is—and always shall be—unacceptable. But when we encounter Jesus in the New Testament, we see He ascribes to Himself all the attributes of deity. Now we have a problem: How do we account for Jesus? Obviously, because of the teaching of the Old Testament, He cannot be "another" god.

In the telling words of C. S. Lewis from *Mere Christianity*, Jesus claimed to be God, and only three possibilities exist to explain that claim:

1. Jesus knew He was not God, making Him a liar;
2. Jesus thought He was God, but wasn't, making Him a lunatic; or
3. Jesus actually is God, as He claimed, making Him the Lord.

Some people argue that Jesus is a prophet, a good man or a great teacher—but not God. That really isn't possible. If His claims are not true, they are horrendous. He must be either a liar, a lunatic or the Lord.

Is Jesus God?

To establish the *biblical* proof for the full deity of Jesus, we need only look at the texts that support that claim. We will look at texts that support His omnipresence, omnipotence and omniscience. In addition, we will see that He is called God and Creator, and that He receives worship.

Jesus Is Omnipresent

Jesus articulates an amazing fact in Matthew 18:20: "Where two or three are gathered together in My name, I am there in the midst of them." This "indwelling" of Christ in the life of the disciple is more than a platitude. It is more than a nice idea or a symbolic statement. Paul tells us it is at the very root of the relationship God establishes with believers. He calls it the Christian "mystery": "To [Christians] God willed to make known what are the riches of the glory of this mystery among the Gentiles: which is Christ in you, the hope of glory" (Colossians 1:27).

Jesus further declares His omnipresence when He speaks with Nicodemus. Jesus, telling Nicodemus about his need to be born again, remarks that though Nicodemus is an influential Jew, he is ignorant of spiritual things. Commenting on His omniscience, Jesus says:

> "If I have told you earthly things and you do not believe, how will you believe if I tell you heavenly things? No one has ascended to heaven but He who came down from heaven, that is, the Son of Man who is in heaven. John 3:12–13

Again, at His ascension Jesus states that He will always be with the disciples "even to the end of the age" (Matthew 28:20). Likewise, on the night of Jesus' betrayal He has a long talk with the disciples. He says in "a little while longer," the world will not see Him, but the disciples will see Him. As a matter of fact, because He lives, they will live. And they will know that He is *in* them (John 14:19–20).

Yes, the very real presence of Christ dwelling in believers throughout the world is a magnificent demonstration of His omnipresence. Shortly after I became a Christian it dawned on me that the Person Jesus Christ was literally with me. The testimony of all born-again Christians is the testimony of Paul:

> I have been crucified with Christ; it is no longer I who live, but Christ lives in me; and the life which I now live in the flesh I live by faith in the Son of God, who loved me and gave Himself for me.   Galatians 2:20

Jesus Is Omnipotent

Jesus demonstrates His omnipotence by healing the sick, raising the dead and taking authority over the wind and the waves. While it could be argued that the disciples would later do similar miracles, Jesus claims He has this power "within Himself." The disciples' power is but a mere extension of His own. All power and authority reside in Him; it is He who answers the prayers of the disciples who pray "in His name."

Jesus exhibits the power of life and death. To the Jews He says: "No one takes [My life] from Me, but I lay it down of Myself. I have power to lay it down, and I have power to take it again" (John 10:18).

After His resurrection Jesus reveals this power over life and death to John: "I am He who lives, and was dead, and behold, I am alive forevermore. Amen. And I have the keys of Hades and of Death" (Revelation 1:18).

Again in the book of Revelation He says: "I am the Alpha and the Omega, the Beginning and the End. I will give of the fountain of the water of life freely to him who thirsts" (Revelation 21:6).

Jesus Is Omniscient

One of the best examples of Jesus' omniscience is found in John chapter one. Philip, already selected by Jesus as a disciple, says to his friend Nathanael: "We have found Him of whom Moses in the law, and also the prophets, wrote—Jesus of Nazareth, the son of Joseph." Nathanael is unimpressed. He is also a skeptic. He asks, "Can anything good come out of Nazareth?"

Still, he follows Philip to where Jesus is. Jesus, seeing him coming, says, "Behold, an Israelite indeed, in whom is no guile!"

Nathanael then asks Him how He knew him. Jesus replies that He saw Nathanael—before Philip called him—under the very fig tree where Nathanael had been sitting. This knowledge is so astounding to Nathanael that he replies, "Rabbi, You are the Son of God! You are the King of Israel!" (John 1:45–49).

This ability to see something not immediately present goes much deeper: He can see into people's very souls. The Bible says that as the people start to believe on Jesus' name, He does not "commit Himself to them." This is because "He knew all men, and had no need that anyone should testify of man, for He knew what was in man" (John 2:23–25).

In other words, Jesus needs no information about anyone's character, because He has it already, within Him. This is clearly demonstrated when the disciples murmur about Jesus' "hard" sermon about eating His flesh and drinking His blood. Many of the disciples leave Him over this saying. Even the Twelve are troubled by it. The Bible says Jesus "knew in Himself" they were murmuring (John 6:61). Further, Jesus knows beforehand who will ultimately believe in Him: "For

Jesus knew from the beginning who they were who did not believe, and who would betray Him" (John 6:64).

Jesus describes Himself as the Being who "has eyes like a flame of fire" (Revelation 2:18).

Jesus Is Worshiped as God

As firmly as the Jews understood there was only one God, so they understood that only God receives worship. Idolatry is the worship of anything or any being other than God and is clearly condemned throughout the Old Testament. Yet it is a trap God's people have fallen into repeatedly down through the ages.

Jesus leaves no doubt about worship belonging to God alone: "You shall worship the Lord your God, and Him only shall you serve" (Matthew 4:10). At the same time Jesus allows people to worship Him. He *receives* worship. When Jesus heals a blind man, the Jewish leaders chastise the man and cast him out of the synagogue. When Jesus hears that, He finds the man and asks him, "Do you believe in the Son of God?" The man replies, "Lord, I believe!" and worships Him. At which Jesus says: "For judgment I have come into this world, that those who do not see may see, and that those who see may be made blind" (John 9:35, 38–39).

Other stories abound. Jesus goes walking across the sea one night and meets the disciples in their boat. Once He is aboard, they worship Him (Matthew 14:24–33).

In one of the most touching stories in the Bible, a Syro-Phoenician woman worships Jesus as she entreats Him to heal her daughter. Jesus commends her as a woman of great faith (Matthew 15:22–28).

Jesus is worshiped by the disciples at His ascension (Luke 24:52); by the 24 elders in heaven (Revelation 5:8–10); by angels (Revelation 5:12); by all creatures:

> And every creature which is in heaven and on the earth and under the earth and such as are in the sea, and all that are in them, I heard saying: "Blessing and honor and glory and power be to Him who sits on the throne, and to the Lamb, forever and ever!"   Revelation 5:13

Jesus will be worshiped ultimately by everyone, saint and sinner alike: For every knee shall bow and every tongue shall confess that Jesus Christ is Lord (Philippians 2:10–11).

Jesus Is Called God

In the Old Testament Isaiah prophesies the incarnation (literally, *enfleshment*) of God in Christ:

> "Behold, the virgin shall conceive and bear a Son, and shall call His name Immanuel. . . ." For unto us a Child is born, unto us a Son is given; and the government will be upon His shoulder. And His name will be called Wonderful, Counselor, Mighty God, Everlasting Father, Prince of Peace.   Isaiah 7:14; 9:6

This promise is fulfilled in the birth of Jesus. Matthew tells us Jesus, the Son of Mary, is none other than "God with us" (Matthew 1:23).

John says: "In the beginning was the Word, and the Word was with God, and the Word was God" (John 1:1).

According to John 1:14, "The Word became flesh and dwelt

among us, and we beheld His glory." First Timothy 3:16 says that "God was manifested in the flesh."

Thomas the doubter refused to believe that Jesus had been resurrected. Eight days later, when Jesus walked through the walls of the room in which the disciples were meeting and told Thomas to put his hands in the sword wound in His side and the nail wounds in His hands, Thomas replied, "My Lord and my God!" (John 20:28).

Colossians 2:9–10 tells us that in Jesus "dwells all the fullness of the Godhead bodily." That is a complete statement about Jesus' divine nature. Titus 2:13 calls Him "our great God and Savior Jesus Christ."

In explaining the nature of Jesus, Hebrews 1:3 says Jesus is the brightness of God's glory, the exact representation of His being. In other words, Jesus is what we can see of God.

We are finite; we cannot see throughout the universe. God is infinite. He is omnipresent, existing throughout the universe. What we can see of God is what He reveals to us. The best revelation of His infinity is in the God-Man, Jesus. That is why John says no one has seen God at any time, except as the Son has revealed Him (John 1:18). God Himself in speaking to this mystery of the incarnation of Christ says to His son, "Your throne, O God, is forever and ever" (Hebrews 1:8).

Jesus calls Himself "the First and the Last" (Revelation 1:17–18). Elsewhere He says: "He who overcomes shall inherit all things, and I will be his God and he shall be My son" (Revelation 21:7).

Jesus Is the Creator

We understand that the definition of God includes the description of Him as the Creator—or First Cause, as the early philosophers put it. Genesis 1:1 says, "In the beginning God created the heavens and the earth." John specifically identifies the Creator God as Jesus: "All things were made through Him, and without Him nothing was made that was made. In Him was life" (John 1:3–4).

In Colossians, Paul reiterates the creative nature of Jesus. First, he explains that Jesus is what we can see of God: "He is the image of the invisible God." Then he says:

> For by Him all things were created that are in heaven and that are on earth, visible and invisible, whether thrones or dominions or principalities or powers. All things were created through Him and for Him. And He is before all things, and in Him all things consist.
>
> Colossians 1:15–17

Hebrews 1:10 says Jesus laid the foundations of the earth and calls heaven the work of His hands.

The full deity of Jesus is the doctrinal line the Church has drawn historically, marking the boundary of minimum faith for a true Christian. It is impossible to have a vibrant faith in Christ if He is merely a great moral teacher, a Spirit-filled man or even the Son of God without being fully God. The very essence of the cults is their rebellion against this revelation of God.

The Trinity

The doctrine of the holy Trinity is the doctrinal formulation the Church has consistently advanced in the face of the heretic. The concept of the Trinity seeks basically to encapsulate what the Bible says about God in both the Old and New Testaments.

The Old Testament forever establishes the fact that, in all the universe, only one God exists. The battle against paganism in the Old Testament was Israel's defense of the one God against the polytheism of the Gentiles. The Old Testament prophets chastise Israel continually for following the detestable practices of the Gentiles in "whoring after false gods." The problem arises for some when, once we have the light of monotheism burning brightly from the Old Testament witness, we are confronted with Jesus' claim to Godhood in the New Testament.

How do we explain the Person of Jesus in the Trinity?

1. We refute the idea that Jesus is another god. That thinking is precluded by the Old Testament. That is why tritheism—the most frequent error of the cults (such as Mormonism or Jehovah's Witnesses)—is unacceptable. Tritheism calls for three separate gods: one god who is the Father, one god who is the Son and one god who is the Holy Spirit.

2. We refute the idea that Jesus is less than God. Where tritheism emphasizes the "threeness" of God, Unitarianism emphasizes the "oneness" of God. Unitarianism relegates Jesus to the role of being—not an eternal Person who both is God and is with God (John 1:1), but a manifestation of God. Jesus becomes another burning bush or pillar of cloud. God is not big enough; therefore, He must somehow stop being Father to become Son.

The doctrine of the Trinity allows Jesus to share the one nature of God without confusion or dissolution. Hence the one God is eternally Father, Son and Holy Spirit. If this is not true, Jesus came into existence at some point in time and is, therefore, not eternal, not God.

The cults are indeed the "unpaid bills of the Church."

There was a time when a solid Christian, raised up in C. H. Spurgeon's church or D. L. Moody's church, would have been expert in the doctrine of the Trinity. He or she would have been forced to think through the doctrinal ramifications of it. Likewise, we must become familiar with the scriptural revelation of the nature of God in order to walk the cultist through the biblical proofs for the full deity of Christ.

Section 4
Liberating Hard
Cases

14
The Power of the Gospel Message

Chuck Colson and Francis Shaeffer were right. We live in a post-Christian society that truly is the new Dark Ages. The return to paganism, which began in the Enlightenment, is nearly complete: The secularists are content that God is dead; the cultists think only they know God; the occultists think everything is God. Of the three, perhaps the occultists will preside over the sad end of mankind. A reading of Matthew 24 and the book of Revelation could suggest that.

Still, optimistic voices are heard. Some Christians predict a great "last days" revival. Many look to the fall of Soviet Communism as an opportunity for world evangelism. Others hope the failure of Communism's materialistic philosophy will force the world to reconsider Western theism. Conservative educators like John Silber, president of Boston University, hope for a moral reawakening in America. Finally, believing scientists hope the newest discoveries, both on the sub-atomic and the astronomical levels, will cause the world to acknowledge the presence of God at the center of the universe.

I'm ambivalent. Try as I might, I can't detect a meaningful move away from the brink. That does not make me pessimistic, because the certain eventual outpouring of God's wrath will result in the permanent cleansing of the earth from all the lies of the devil. More important, I feel that my part in God's plan is the same regardless of whether civilization remains for one or one hundred more years. How and when God brings the Kingdom to pass is His prerogative as manager of the cosmos; I am simply committed to proclaiming His Lordship. I pray God's Kingdom will come so that His will can be done on earth as it is in heaven.

I do not despair. I go for small gains wherever I can. I believe the souls of His children are of great worth to God and I work to light the Gospel candle in a dark world. Evangelical success is not measured in terms of numbers, but of faithfulness. I want to be faithful to the Great Commission.

The theme in this book is simple: Our responsibility to those who are snared in secularism, cultism and occultism is to help disentangle them from Satan's philosophical lies. Only then will they be able to hear the Gospel message.

After the devil's fingers are removed from his victim's ears, the Gospel must be declared. Only the Gospel message is freighted with the power to reconcile mankind to God.

The One-Two Punch

An example of the one-two punch of apologetics followed by declaration is found in the conversion of the apostle Paul. Paul (who was known as Saul of Tarsus before his conversion) was a great enemy of embryonic Christianity. He was a contemporary of Jesus, probably a rabbinic student in Jerusalem during Jesus' three-year ministry. He was a Pharisee, a knowledgeable Jewish leader. Beyond that, he was an active opponent of Christianity: He was present at, and gladly consented to, the stoning of Stephen, the first martyr of the Church; he was a ferocious antagonist of the Church, who "made havoc of the church, entering every house, and dragging off men and women, committing them to prison" (Acts 7:58; 8:1, 3).

Paul was converted during a miraculous intervention of God. On his way to Damascus with a pocketful of warrants to arrest Christians, he encountered the risen Jesus. He fell to his feet and was blinded. A voice from heaven said, "Saul, Saul, why are you persecuting Me?"

"Who are You, Lord?" Paul asked.

"I am Jesus, whom you are persecuting. It is hard for you to kick against the goads." (See Acts 9:1–9.)

The Damascus road vision is, I believe, misunderstood to be the sum total of Paul's conversion experience—as though it happened in a vacuum! On the contrary, I believe it was the *culmination of years of hard case witnessing* to Paul.

The Bible indicates Paul had abundant contact with Christians *prior* to his Damascus road vision. He would have heard numerous sermons by the Christian disciples in his attempts to suppress their teaching. Besides Stephen's preaching, he may well have heard Peter and other apostles, or even Jesus Himself. He probably argued with the upstart apostates. (In fact, anyone familiar with Paul can hardly imagine that he *didn't.*) Certainly, as he pursued his zealous persecution of the Church, he thought deeply about what he saw and heard; we know his analytical character from his extensive writings in the New Testament epistles. The Damascus road vision was, therefore, in my opinion, the second part of the hard case formula. It was the final declaration of the Gospel on the heels of much apologetic ministry.

I can verify that miraculous revelation often follows the apologetic work done by God's ministers. On numerous occasions people I have witnessed to have related to me that after our heated discussions something "occurred" to them, that God "spoke" to them. This communication normally is not in a vision like Paul's, but it is often just as dramatic and life-changing to the recipient. The Gospel message, when delivered to opened ears, still has the power to change lives just as it did in the first century.

My wife, Margaretta, testifies that only after she had been soundly challenged about Mormon salvation, which is dependent upon "good works," did God reveal Himself to her. In her thirty years of intense commitment to Mormonism, she had never heard the Gospel of salvation by grace through faith. Shortly after being confronted with the works vs. grace issue, she walked into a strange home and saw a "miraculous" Scripture verse taped to a mirror: "For by grace you have been saved through faith, and that not of yourselves; it is the gift of God, not of works, lest anyone should boast" (Ephesians 2:8–9).

Margaretta remembers it as an emotional moment for her. She said she knew it was no accident that she saw the verse. It was a radical confirmation to her that God was personally interested in her and involved in her life. We should not be surprised that this type of revelation follows preaching, since the Bible declares "signs" follow faith, which follows preaching (Mark 16:15–18).

The Bible teaches that God works hand in hand with His servants to bring others to salvation. While the Bible indeed says, "Whoever calls on the name of the Lord shall be saved," it links calling upon God with confrontive declaration:

> "Whoever calls on the name of the Lord shall be saved." How then shall they call on Him in whom they have not believed? And how shall they believe in Him of

whom they have not heard? And how shall they hear without a preacher? And how shall they preach unless they are sent?   Romans 10:13–15

Christian essayist G. K. Chesterton talked about confrontation in this way:

> There is a notion abroad that to win a man we must agree with him. Actually, the opposite is true. Each generation has had to be converted by the man who contradicted it most. The man who is going in a wrong direction will never be set right by the affable religionist who falls into step beside him and goes the same way. Someone must place himself across the path and insist that the straying man turn around and go in the right direction.

Once God (usually through His witnesses) has penetrated the fog of the devil's lies, the simple declaration of the Gospel message is powerful. When that message falls on an opened heart, it is as if a seed of the Kingdom of God takes root and grows (Mark 4:3–20). It is so powerful, in fact, that Jesus said it grows "all by itself": "The kingdom of God is as if a man should scatter seed on the ground, and should sleep by night and rise by day, and the seed should sprout and grow, he himself does not know how" (Mark 4:26–27).

Paul always marveled at the impact of the conversion experience. It was a complete transformation. He called it a conveyance or transferring from one kingdom to another, a resurrection from death to life (Colossians 1:13; Ephesians 2:5). Paul also understood the immediacy of the impact of the Gospel on an opened heart. His own conversion was apocalyptic. He would later describe it not as a learning experience, but as *revelation*.

Often hard cases look "impossible" to us: Those who are being saved out of the webs of satanic lies don't always appear to be good candidates for conversion. I have a friend who was converted to Christ out of an occult group led by Bhagwan Shree Rajaneesh. The young man attended an evangelistic meeting under duress from his parents. Dressed in the typical bright orange garb of his discipleship, he wasn't interested in "finding Christ." In fact, he was tired of the discussions with his parents. But the meeting was orchestrated by God. The words of the evangelist, in concert with the previous hard case witnessing, untied his foggy, occult thinking. That night my friend changed kingdoms. He was born again.

The lesson? When we engage the devil's victims in what appears to be fruitless dialogue, God may be working strongly, even when we think He isn't. When we dialogue, they win; when we don't, they lose. *Don't stop short.*

Paul said of his own experience that he came to Christ "when it pleased God . . . to reveal His Son in me" (Galatians 1:15–16). The word *reveal* in that passage is the same word that transliterates into our word *apocalypse.* Paul's explosive moment of revelation came at the culmination of a process known only to God.

Fight the Good Fight of Faith

I certainly do not understand the process of salvation. I can't make it happen for anyone. I can't open a person's mind and force the Gospel in. I am left, ultimately, to my part of the process—sales. I declare. I am a witness. If you are a disciple, you are a witness.

It is a noble calling, this call to the Great Commission. And a taxing one. I commend you to the task of witnessing to hard cases, of winning "impossibles" for Christ. I charge you to keep the faith, run a good race, fight the good fight of faith. And remember: "Let us not grow weary while doing good, for in due season we shall reap if we do not lose heart" (Galatians 6:9).

15
Thinking It Through:

Questions for personal reflection and group dialogue

Chapter 1

1. Define a hard case.
2. How does God want us to view hard cases?
3. Where do hard case philosophies originate?
4. What are the three categories of hard cases? What is the philosophical basis for each category?
5. What are the predominant kinds of hard cases in your community?
6. What are some of the excuses you would give for not reaching hard cases? How would God answer those excuses?
7. Give examples, if any, of attempts to win a hard case that failed. Why do you think that failure happened?

Chapter 2

1. What are some examples of "evil ideas" and their consequences?

2. What are some of the "evil ideas" you have bought into in the past? What was their effect on you?

3. How did you escape from these ideas and effects?

4. What keeps hard cases from hearing the Gospel?

5. Knowing that our primary conflict is with the forces of hell, what should a Christian do to be prepared for those conflicts?

Chapter 3

1. Discuss the differences between relational, declarational and confrontational evangelism.

2. Why is confrontational evangelism necessary?

3. Why is confrontational evangelism difficult for the Christian?

4. How is confrontational evangelism an act of love?

5. How do we confront the three types of hard cases: secularists, cultists and occultists?

6. Give some personal examples of confrontational evangelism and its effects.

Chapter 4

1. Why is there a reluctance about hard case witnessing in the Christian community?

2. How should a Christian feel about another Christian who is reluctant to try hard case witnessing?

3. What motivates you to witness to hard cases?

4. What are some examples from the Bible for hard case witnessing?

Chapter 5

1.   Identify the primary characteristics of secularists, cultists and occultists.

2.   What do these three categories of hard cases have in common?

3.   What is your job and what is God's job in a hard case encounter?

Chapter 6

1.   What are the lessons we can learn from the Tower of Babel? How does this relate to those who hold to hard case philosophies?

2.   What can we learn from the fall of Satan and the fall of man in relation to those who hold to hard case philosophies?

3.   How have Western and Eastern paganism influenced modern hard case philosophies?

4.   How has secularism opened a door for cultism and occultism in our society?

5.   Why is it important to grasp the basics of biblical revelation?

Chapter 7

1.   Why has atheism not done well in historic thought?

2.   Why have there been alternatives to God's revelation in the Bible?

3.   What forces produced the Enlightenment?

4.   When and why did thinkers start predominantly to question creation?

5. Do you see a planned historic plot from Satan to distract mankind from the revelation of God? What does this say to you?

6. How are secular influences manifested and promoted in your community?

Chapter 8

1. How was the theory of evolution developed?

2. What is the key to reaching the secularist?

3. Why is the view of theistic evolution important to know when dealing with a secularist?

4. In what ways have you been influenced by the theory of evolution?

5. If the theory of evolution is more of a philosophy than a science, why does it persist?

Chapter 9

1. Why is secularism actually a religion?

2. Why is it important to confront a secularist with the error of the theory of evolution?

3. What is the goal in helping a secularist see the error of the theory of evolution?

4. Where do you take him once he honestly questions his belief in the theory of evolution?

Chapter 10

1. How are Hinduism and modern occultism like Old Testament idolatry?

2. What is the aim of witchcraft?

3. What is the New Age movement?

4. How has our recent history ushered in the onslaught of occult philosophy?

5. Describe the different systems that promote occult thinking and practice in your community.

6. How should a Christian prepare to witness to a person trapped in the hard case philosophy of the occult?

Chapter 11

1. What is the method for reaching the occultist?

2. Why should we be confrontational when dealing with those in the occult?

3. What benefit is there in exposing the nature of occultists' hidden teachings and practices?

4. When dealing with the occultist, how can we protect ourselves spiritually?

5. What are some diagnostic questions we can ask in determining if we are dealing with an occult philosophy?

Chapter 12

1. What is the definition of a cult?

2. Why do you have to watch out for religious words when dealing with a person in a cult?

3. What is "cultishness"? Can one be a Christian and yet be a cultist?

4. Why is it important to be able to distinguish between a full-blown cult and people who are cultish in certain beliefs?

5. What is the sure mark of a cult?

6. How can you prepare yourself for dealing with a person in a cult?

Chapter 13

1. Discuss the three primary aspects of God: His omni-science, His omnipotence and His omnipresence.

2. State, in simple terms, the doctrine of the Trinity.

3. Why does a cult try to disprove the divinity of Jesus?

4. How should you present the fact of the deity of Jesus to a cult member?

To contact James R. Spencer or to receive the newsletter *Through the Maze* write:

James R. Spencer
Through the Maze
P.O. Box 8656
Boise, ID 83707

Bibliography

Books

Bowden, M. *Ape Men—Fact or Fallacy?* Bromely, Kent, Canada: Sovereign Publications, 1977.

Butterfield, Herbert. *Christianity and History*. London: Collings/Fontana, 1957.

Colson, Chuck. *Against the Night: Living in the New Dark Ages*. Ann Arbor, Mich.: Servant Publications, 1989.

Conway, Flo and Siegelman, Jim. *Snapping*. New York: Dell, 1979.

Cook, Jean and Kramer, Ann. *History's Timeline*. London: Grisewood & Dempsey, Ltd., 1981.

Decker, J. Edward. *The Question of Freemasonry*. Issaquah, Wash.: *Saints Alive!*, 1985.

Darwin, Charles. *On the Origin of Species*. London: J. M. Dent and Sons, Ltd., 1971.

Dowley, Tim (editor). *Eerdman's Handbook to the History of Christianity*. Grand Rapids, Mich.: Wm. B. Eerdmans Publishing Co., 1977.

Eldredge, Niles. *Time Frames: The Rethinking of Darwinian Evolution and the Theory of Punctuated Equilibria*. New York: Simon and Schuster, 1985.

Ferguson, Marilyn. *The Aquarian Conspiracy*. Boston: Houghton Mifflin Co., 1980.

Fix, William. *The Bone Peddlers*. New York: Macmillan Publishing Co., 1984.

Gish, Duane. *Evolution, the Fossils Say No!* San Diego: Master Books, 1981.

Hall, Manly P. *The Secret Teachings of all Ages*. Los Angeles: The Philosophical Research Society, Inc., 1971.

—*The Mystical Christ*. Los Angeles: The Philosophical Research Society, Inc., 1951.

—*Reincarnation the Cycle of Necessity*. Los Angeles: The Philosophical Research Society, Inc., 1967.

Hawking, Stephen. *A Brief History of Time*. New York: Bantam, 1988.

Hilary of Poitiers. *On the Trinity*, 2.2 (as cited in Brown, Harold, O. J. *Heresies*. Garden City, N.Y.: Doubleday, 1984.

Hoyle, Sir Fred and Wickramasinghe, Chandra. *Evolution from Space*. London: J. M. Dent & Sons, Ltd., 1981.

Hokema, Anthony A. *The Four Major Cults*. Grand Rapids, Mich.: William B. Eerdmans, Publishing Co., 1963.

Houghton, S. M. *Sketches from Church History*. Edinburgh, Scotland: The Banner of Truth Trust, 1980.

Hunt, Dave and McMahon, T. A. *The Sorcerer's New Apprentice*. Eugene, Or.: Harvest House Publ. 1988.

Huse, Scott M. *The Collapse of Evolution*. Grand Rapids, Mich.: Baker Book House, 1983.

Kerut, G. A. *Implications of Evolution*. London: Pergamon Press, 1960.

Larson, Bob. *Straight Answers on the New Age*. Nashville: Thomas Nelson Publishers, 1989.

Lever, Ruth. *Acupuncture for Everyone*. New York.: Penguin Books, 1987.

Lewis, Gordon R. and Demarest, Bruce A. *Integrative Theology*

Volumes I & II. Grand Rapids, Mich.: Zondervan Publishing House, 1990.

Manchester, William. *The Last Lion*. New York.: Dell Publishing, 1983.

McDowell, Josh. *Evidence That Demands a Verdict*. Arrowhead Springs, Calif.: Campus Crusade for Christ, Inc., 1972.

Milton, John. *Paradise Lost*. Chicago.: Encyclopaedia Britannica, 1952.

Nilsson, Heribert. *Synthetische Artbildung*. Lund, Sweden: Verlag CWE Gleerup, 1954.

Prophet, Elizabeth Clare. *The Lost Years of Jesus*. Livingston, Mt.: Summit University Press, 1972.

Schaeffer, Francis. *The Great Evangelical Disaster*. Westchester, Ill.: Crossway Books, 1984.

Sackett, Chuck. *What's Going On in There?* Thousand Oaks, Calif.: Sword of the Shepherd Ministries, Inc., 1982.

Schlossberg, Herbert. *Idols for Destruction*. Nashville: Thomas Nelson Publishers, 1983.

Schnoebelen, William and Spencer, James R. *Mormonism's Temple of Doom*. Boise, Id.: Triple J Publishers, 1987.

—*Whited Sepulchers*. Boise, Id.: Triple J Publishers, 1990.

Spencer, James R., *Have You Witnessed to a Mormon Lately?* Tarrytown, N.Y.: Chosen Books, 1986.

Sunderland, Luther D. *Darwin's Enigma*. Santee, Calif.: Master Book Publishers, 1984.

Tuthill, Paul. *Subliminal Success Tapes and Accessories Catalog*. Grand Rapids, Mich.: Mind Communication, Inc., 1990.

Waite, Arthur Edward. *A New Encyclopaedia of Freemasonry, Vol. 1*. New York.: Weathervane Books, 1970.

Wells, H. G. *The Outline of History*. Garden City, N.Y.: Doubleday & Company, Inc., 1971.

Yogi, Maharishi Mahesh. *Transcendental Meditation*. New York: Signet Books, 1968.

Zuckerman, Sir Solly. *Beyond the Ivory Tower*. New York: Taplinger Pub. Co., 1980.

Encyclopedia and Anthologies

Abrams, M. H. (general editor). *The Norton Anthology of English Literature*. New York: W. W. Norton and Company, Inc., 1962.

Garraty, John A. and Gay, Peter (general editors). *The Columbia History of the World*. New York: Harper & Row, Publishers, 1981.

NIV Study Bible. Grand Rapids, Mich.: The Zondervan Corporation, 1985.

Snelling, Andrew (editor). *The Revised Quote Book*. Brisbane. Qld.: Creation Science Foundation, Ltd., 1990.

Encyclopaedia Britannica. Chicago: 15th Edition, 1981.
Vol. 5, p. 507
Vol. 6, p. 816
Vol. 7, p. 17
Vol. 8, p. 889
Vol. 9, p. 138
Vol. 14, p. 542

Encyclopedia of Philosophy. New York: Macmillan Publishing Co., Inc., Vol. 8, p. 189.

Audiotapes

Gange, Robert. *God, Man, and the Universe*. Irving, Tex.: Word Inc., 1984.

Periodicals and Other Articles

Anderson, G. M. and Keith, M. L. "Radiocarbon Dating: Fictitious Results with Mollusk Shells." *Science*, Vol. 141, August 16, 1963, pp. 634–635.

Bower, Bruce. "Subliminal Messages: Changes for the Better?" *Science News*, March 8, 1986, p. 156–157.

Eden, Murray. "Inadequacies of New-Darwinian Evolution as a Scientific Theory." *The Wistar Symposium Monograph No. 5*, Philadelphia, Wistar Institute Press, 1967, p. 9.

Ehrlich, Paul. "Evolutionary History and Population Biology." *Nature*, Vol. 214, p. 352.

Goldschmidt, Richard B. "Evolution as Viewed by One Geneticist." *American Scientist*, Vol. 40, January 1952, p. 97.

Gould, Stephen Jay. "Evolution as Fact and Theory." *Discover*, May 1981, p. 37.

—"Is a New and General Theory of Evolution Evolving?" *Paleobiology*, Vol. 6 (1), January 1980, p. 127.

Haddon, David. "Transcendental Meditation Challenges the Church." *Christianity Today*, March 26, 1976, pp. 15–16.

Hoyle, Sir Fred. "Hoyle on Evolution." *Nature*, Vol. 294, p. 105.

Kanner, Bernice. "From the Subliminal to the Ridiculous." *New York*, December 4, 1989, p. 20.

Kitts, David B. "Paleontology and Evolutionary Theory." *Evolution*, Vol. 28, September 28, 1974, p. 467.

Lammerts, William E. "Growing Doubts: Is Evolutionary Theory Valid?" *Christianity Today*, September 14, 1962, p. 4.

Lee, Robert E. "Radiocarbon: Ages in Error." *Anthropological Journal of Canada*, Vol. 19 (3), 1981, pp. 9–29.

Lindsey, Robert. "Guru's Hired to Motivate Workers Are

Raising Fears of 'Mind Control.' " *New York Times*, April 17, 1987.

Moyers, Bill. "Interview: Isaac Asimov." *The Humanist*, January/February 1989, p. 6.

Natalie, Jo Anna. "Are You Open to Suggestion?" *Psychology Today*, September 1988, p. 28.

Lofton, John. "John Lofton's Journal." *The Washington Times*, Feb. 8, 1984.

O'Rourke, J. E. "Pragmatism Versus Materialism in Stratigraphy." *American Journal of Science*, Vol. 276, January 1976, p. 47.

Reader, John. "Whatever Happened to Zinjanthropus?" *New Scientist*, March 26, 1981, p. 802.

Riggs, Alan C. "Major Carbon-14 Deficiency in Modern Snail Shells from Southern Nevada Springs." *Science*, Vol. 224, April 6, 1984, p. 58.

Wald, George. "The Origins of Life." *Scientific American*, Vol. 191 (2), p. 48.

Watson, Lyall. "The Water People." *Science Digest*, Vol. 90, May 1982, p. 44.

Willis, Tom. "Lucy Goes to College." *CSA News*, February 1987.

White Tim. "Hominid Collarbone Exposed As Dolphin's Rib." *New Scientist*, April 28, 1983, p. 199.